Fishcamp

by
Dorothy Savage Joseph

ISBN 0-89288-270-0

Library of Congress Catalog Card Number: 97-94052

Printed by
Maverick Publications • P.O. Box 5007 • Bend, Oregon 97708

Table of Contents

Special thanks to:

Ellen Savage (mom) for her shared memories.

Rose (Newman) Vaska and Sister Kathleen (Margaret Cantwell) for sharing pictures.

My son Mark for lending me his computer, printer and his patience in helping me use them.

Introduction

I'm dedicating this book to my paternal grandparents, Nikolai and Aneska Savage, who found our "Fishcamp" and lived there, year round for several years, with their families in the early 1940's. I'm writing this, to share with you, the happy memories of living in fishcamp. Memories full of fun and work. When we lived there as children, it seemed like a lonesome and at times boring place to be. Now I realize there is no place to live that can compare with the peacefulness, serenity and satisfaction of living in "Fishcamp".

Even though this book is called "Fishcamp", I'm including in it, other parts of my life in the village of Holy Cross, Alaska and travels on the rivers surrounding the area.

Grandma Aneska and Grandpa Nikolai (Iya) Savage.
Paternal Grandparents.

Chapter 1

My grandparents, parents, aunts and uncles traveled together, by boat in the summer and dog sled in the winter, to different areas, living in tents or small cabins to hunt, fish, or trap. Different seasons found them in various parts of the Yukon or Innoko River.

Since I was pretty young at that time, the activities I'm telling you about were told to me by mom and dad. They talked a lot about their younger years adventures together.

Grandma and Grandpa Savage were very special people to me. I remember them a little, as I was about five years old at the time of their deaths in the late 1940's.

Grandpa was a very dark fierce looking Athabascan man. The only recollection of him I had was of him walking with a cane. He would also be sitting on the floor in the small cabin in Holy Cross, working on his dog harnesses or sled. His name was Nikolai Savage, but had the Indian name of "Iya".

Grandpa was from the village of Nikolai, Alaska. He was known by his Indian name, until the missionaries gave him the name of Nikolai Savage. The last name was given to refer to his fierceness.

He was known to be a powerful medicine man and practiced his shaman abilities on anyone needing his care. He worked hard fishing, trapping, hunting, wood cutting to provide food and clothes for his family.

In his younger days with grandma, they lived in a small village across and below the present Holy Cross village site. This was called Red Wing. Here many people lived to cut wood to sell to the local store keeper in that village. The storekeeper told my grandparents that when he died, he wanted my auntie to have the village because she was born there. The village eventually died out as all the people moved away to different villages. Some moved to Holy Cross, and Piamute. Piamute was another village located about 30 miles below Holy Cross and about 5 miles below our present fishcamp.

All the people there eventually moved away and it now belongs to a family as their fishcamp.

Grandma Aneska Savage (left), her sister Grandma Tasiana Demientieff (right) and cousin Theresa in front. Taken in the 1930's.

Grandma Aneska was born in a small village somewhere along the Kuskokwim river. This village has long since been abandoned and the location is not known. Her father was from Russia, her mother was an Eskimo lady from the area.

Grandma was a special kind person to me. The time I remember her, we were living in Holy Cross in our small cabins located at the lower end of the village. Her cabin was across the small yard facing ours.

At times, I visited her, watching her work as she sat on the floor by one of the two small windows. Daily she would scrape on skins as she finished the process of curing them. She had this skin scraper, a metal blade attached to a curved wooden handle. She held this and scraped away, and worked the skin until it was smooth and soft. With the different skins, she would sew mukluks and other clothes, while sitting at her favorite spot on the floor.

Mom told me about a fish skin mukluk that grandma made for dad. He wore it to hunting and walking in wet rainy or Spring weather. The skins shoes would keep his feet dry. Anyway, once while hunting, his skin shoes were wet so dad set them by the fire to dry. He had left them too close to the fire and they became over dry causing them to be small and real hard when he tried to put the shoes on the next day.

When visiting grandma, she would ask me to comb her hair as she sat on the floor in her small cabin. I would gather her thin white hair in my hands and gently comb it and roll the back into a small bun. She wore a thin net over her soft, white hair. What a gentle loving person she was.

Grandma had a small bad habit of chewing tobacco. Grandpa had the same bad habit. They had the leaf tobacco stick that they broke into tiny pieces. They would gather tree punks from the nearby woods and burn the punks making ashes. The ashes would be mixed with the leaf tobacco crumbs, thus making a delicious chew for them. They chewed this stuff and would be so expert at spitting, they would never miss their aim at the small spittoons nearby.

Gathering tree punks for them would be a pass time for us. In their small cabin they would always have a few punks on the floor by the stove.

Grandma had a knack at making great tasting brown sugar candy. She would have a supply in her cupboard covered in a bowl. When I visited her she would share her treasured candy with me. I blame my bad teeth on her and her delicious candy.

She was a great cook, especially at making the well known "Russian Pie". This was a mixture of flaked salmon mixed with rice and onions, between a pie shell, and baked in the oven.

When visiting grandma, she would sometimes talk me into singing for her. I would sing this silly song which she loved. "Oh Where Have You Been Billy Boy". Singing with enthusiasm, I would put my hands on my hips and sing, pointing my hand at my cousin when asking where billy boy had been. Grandma and grandpa would laugh and offer me the brown sugar candy as my reward for the "good song" as they would put it. When visiting her she would tell me "Look in the press and you might find something good". Looking in her wooden box kitchen cupboard, I would find an abundance of her famous brown sugar candy.

Grandma had her favorite cast iron stove that she used for cooking. She took her treasured stove everywhere she traveled by boat. The men would carry the stove into the boat and set it up for use. While traveling up the Innoko River or down toward Fishcamp or surrounding areas for berry picking or hunting, she would be busily cooking meals. When the food was ready, the boat would be pulled to shore and everyone would sit down to share her food.

Anyway, I was so young when they died, but I remember the time and activities of their deaths. I never told anyone how sad I was for my grandma, but I thought of her often and missed her a lot.

A little about my parents also before going into the fishcamp part of my book.

Dad, Pius Savage Sr. was born in Holy Cross, Alaska May 5, 1910. He was baptized at the Catholic mission by the local priest who named him after the Pope. Attending the mission school until the second grade, dad didn't read or write very well, but knew how to sign his name. When dropping out of school, he lived with his parents in the village and surrounding areas when fishing or trapping time was in season.

Dad told stories of working in his younger days, the early 1900's. He worked unloading the "Steam Boat" for .25 a day. Big money then.

Across from the village of Holy Cross about 20 miles below the village there was tundra areas where many reindeer were kept. People lived there caring for the reindeer. As a young man this was one of the activities dad was involved in.

He also worked on freight boats as a pilot traveling on the Innoko river to villages such as Shageluk and Holikachuk. This is how he and mom met.

He took mom to Holy Cross and asked the mission priests to marry them. Since mom was not a catholic, the priest refused. Dad had to do a lot of arguing and threatened to take mom to Flat, Alaska to have the magistrate there, do the wedding. The priests finally relented and married them. In those days the missionaries were very strict and followed their

Pius Savage Sr. (dad) and Ellen (mom) taken in Nikolai, Alaska in 1983. They traveled there to demonstrate Indian dancing for students in the village school. Mukluks (boots) they are wearing were made by mom, Ellen.

Mom and Dad (Ellen and Pius Savage Sr.) taken in the village of Nikolai, Ak. in 1983. The cabin behind them is similar to the one we lived in before Dad made the new house in Holy Cross.

religious rules which one was that the Catholics didn't marry non Catholics.

Dad had many experiences he told us about his younger days.

Before dad and mom met, his parents at one time lived at the "Point". This was a small settlement across the village of Holy Cross on the Yukon river. People lived there seasonally, in tents to do their survival jobs such as hunting, fishing and trapping.

Dad said there was a non native store keeper who was ill and living in the small village at the Point. The store keeper lived in that area for many years but was getting on in his years. He knew he was on his deathbed, but didn't want to die in that area. He wanted to be taken to Anchorage or Fairbanks. There was no radio or any other communication with the outside world at that time in this tiny settlement they were in.

Dad and another villager skated up the Innoko river to Shageluk which was roughly 60 miles from Holy Cross and a little less from the village they were in. They skated until they reached Shageluk where a plane was radioed for to take the old man out of the wilderness. We never knew what happened to him after that.

Dad said as a young man, he would run across the river from the point to Holy Cross to attend weekly dances. After the dance was over, he would run across the river back to the settlement. The distance is roughly ten miles or a little less.

Dad was a self made musician. He was able to play all the musical instruments, which he learned by hearing. He didn't know a thing about musical notes but was expert at playing the guitar, violin, piano, mouth organ and accordion. As small children we would enjoy sitting on the floor listening to his musical ability as he played old waltz and polka tunes.

Mom, Ellen Hunter, was born in Shageluk, Alaska to Jane and Nikolai Hunter, September 18, 1919. She was one of two survivors of the many children her parents had. All seemed to die from different sicknesses that would be around such as TB or who knows what else. In those days, since there were no doctors around, people sometimes didn't know what illnesses they had.

Mom was born at a berry picking camp. At the time of her birth, her grandpa was on a bear hunting trip. Returning he found that he had a new granddaughter. Entering the tent, he took her and brought her to the bear he had just killed. Rubbing her head against the bear, he said she would be like the bear, brave and never afraid of anything.

Her parents were hard workers. Grandpa Hunter was given his name by the local storekeeper because of grandpa's ability to hunt and support his family.

Mom said he always wondered what his real last name was and who his relatives were such as if he had brothers or sisters. There was a family who traveled from the village of Holikachuk, located above Shageluk on the Innoko river. The men would tell mom she was their niece and their dad would tell her he was her grandpa. This made mom wonder if they were his real family and if he should have had their last name. She never asked her parents so we will never know that answer as all the elders who might know the answer are all deceased now.

Like most village people, trapping was Grandpa Hunter's main income. He traveled daily hunting, trapping and fishing and wood cutting. As a small child, she would sometimes accompany him on some of his travels to surrounding areas.

Mom said grandpa would make a canoe out of birch bark. He walked in the woods looking for a long straight birch tree with not much knots. When he found one, he would strip it off the tree and make a canoe out of it, using stripped, split willows to fasten the canoe together. Traveling in the canoe he would keep a can of "pitch" to do emergency repair on leaks the canoe might have.

Mom traveled to many sloughs with grandpa. Sometimes she would see large pikes swimming in the sloughs. She said they were very big and now wondered if they maybe had been alligators. But we decided since she was little at that time, the fish looked to be extra big to her small size.

Mom was raised by her parents in a gentle caring way. Her and my aunt were given everything to make them comfortable and were never out of food or clothing. When grandpa returned from trapping, he would buy them new clothes from the local store. He would supply them with fresh fruit such as oranges when available.

Every fall Grandpa and Grandma would buy a new blanket for her and auntie to use in the cold winter months. They would also be given new reindeer skin for mattress, since they all slept on the floor in their small cabin.

Grandma Hunter followed many old cultural ways which she taught to mom. One event was when girls started their first menstruation. They called this becoming a woman. Mom said she was told to stay in her, sleeping area in the cabin, which would be covered by a curtain. She had to remain behind the curtained area for 20 days. An over parky, gloves, scarf and belt were made for her out of fur and skins. The local medicine woman was called to put these on her and to blow on her. The blowing was part of the ritual girls were treated with when becoming a woman.

She would then have to use the clothes for the next 20 days. She could not leave the curtained area unless she needed to visit the outhouse. She then had to make sure she had the special garments on before leaving the area but had to return to the curtained area as soon as she was finished in the outhouse. Mom said she had to use the parky outfit all summer. She first started her menstruation in the month of April, but had to continue using the outfit even to school. Feeling ashamed for using the clothes, since everyone knew what it meant, she would walk to school by the back roads. The local "meaner" boys would laugh and tease her telling everyone she was "bad luck" woman.

Grandma Hunter (maternal grandma). Taken in the early 1900's in Shageluk, Ak.

Then finally came the time to remove her parky outfit. The medicine man was called for. He then blew on her and removed her parky, scarf, belt and gloves. Grandma made a beaded headband which the medicine man blew on and put on moms head. She had to wear this until the month of August. In August, Grandma then removed the headband and mom was free again. She followed all the strict cultural rules that grandma made her do, even she didn't like them. Her sister was a little more stubborn and didn't follow the rules as well as mom did.

The old medicine man who did his blowing on mom told her "Sathe" which means grandchild, "I blow on you, when I die, I will always watch you. You'll never be hungry and you'll always have something". Mom feels he is still looking after her, even after all the years gone by.

During the time of the first menstruation, grandma told mom not to touch berry bushes. If she did, when she got old her hand and head would be shaky like the bushes. Grandma would pick berries, wash and clean them, putting them over smoke in the smokehouse, before letting mom have the berries.

Another rule was not to pull new grown grass because when she got old her hand would feel like needles were poking at them. She was not to look at the sun because the sun was not good for the eyes. She was to use her scarf at all times because the sun was not good and the heat would give her headaches.

Mom was told not to eat bear meat. This was because the bear was always known to be mean and fierce. Grandma Hunter told mom bear was a very dangerous animal. Anyway mom was always afraid to eat bear meat until after she married dad. One day they were fixing bear meat and when learning mom was afraid to eat it Grandpa Savage took a small piece. He did something to the meat, following his medicine man abilities, and handed it to mom to eat. He told her she was never to be afraid to eat bear meat again and was to share everything they ate from then on. Thus ended her fear of that food.

Grandma Hunter guarded mom and auntie against sicknesses that they might get from someone else. Her and auntie had a special plate and cup for their own use. Their cups were marked by a red and blue yarn tied to the handles. These were the only ones they were allowed to use. Grandma told mom many people came to their house to eat and some of them had TB or other diseases. To guard her children against the diseases, she set aside the special plates and cups. Grandma would wash mom and auntie's cups and dishes in clean hot water before she washed other dishes. She was very strict in protecting them from the diseases.

Many people had tuberculosis which was like an epidemic in those days. Some didn't even know they had it until they started coughing and when in the advanced stages would spit up blood which told them they were in the advanced stages. Many times when people died, villagers didn't know what they died from. Except for tuberculosis, because everyone learned the signs of that disease. They probably didn't know the name of it but knew the symptoms.

Mom attended the local school to the eighth grade. She was taught by non native teachers, who were very strict and sometimes mean toward the local school children. Mom told us children were not allowed to use their native language in school. At times, for the sake of defiance, she would speak her language. She was promptly spanked by the teachers for doing this.

Mom lived in Shageluk until she was sixteen when she met and married dad. She moved to Holy Cross with him and lived there to the time the family moved to Anchorage, Alaska in 1970.

When mom and dad married, as I mentioned before she was not of the catholic religion. A local woman took mom under her "wings" and taught her the religion. She taught mom so strictly, that being a young child not knowledgeable in the evils of the devil, and hearing about his evil deeds, mom was so afraid of evil that she followed the religion strictly, even to this day. Her strong belief in her faith and religion has carried her through many hurts and sorrows.

Dad was working on the freight boat that traveled on the Innoko river when he and mom met. Dances were held in which dad was chosen to be the musician. One of the men paid him fifty cents a song to keep playing all night for dances. Mom said this was how they met. Dad once gave her a box of gum. She still chews that same brand. I guess that box of gum led to marriage and fifteen children, over forty grandchildren and at least thirteen great grandchildren.

Chapter 2

It was before I was born that, my paternal grandparents, with their families, during many of their relocation travels, found the site of our present fishcamp.

It is located on the banks of the Yukon river, about 25 - 30 miles below the village of Holy Cross, Alaska. Surrounded by mountains, it nestles in a small valley with a bubbling creek between one of the mountains and the camp. The Yukon river flows down in front of the camp. Across our camp was a small island separating us from the main channel of the Yukon River.

The small creek, next to our camp, provided us with fresh, cold, clear drinking water that flowed swiftly down from the mountain next to our small house. It was a treat to have the clear cold water, so we wouldn't have to use the Yukon river water or carry water from a distance.

There was a small well worn and used path from our house to the creek. The water was carried in buckets and stored in a larger container kept in the house.

We sometimes stored fresh meat in the creek water to keep the meat from spoiling in the summer heat.

On hot days we used the cold water to wash our hair, ourselves or soaked our feet in it to cool off.

In front of our fishcamp was the Yukon river. As the river flowed swiftly downriver, it was magical and peaceful to sit on the bank watching the river go by. We could tell when the river was rising by the many logs, trees and other objects floating by.

Sometimes a dry log would float by that was good for wood or to use for building logs. My parents would quickly take the boat out and tying a rope to the log would then pull it to shore.

One year, when the men were out, we saw a long straight log floating by. Mom thought it would be good to use for the smoke house. We quickly took the row boat and went downriver after the log. My sisters and mom had to row pretty fast to catch up to the log. Reaching it, a rope was tied to one end of it, and we proceeded to row upriver, back to the fishcamp. When dad returned, he was real proud of our accomplishment.

During World War II my parents lived year round in the fish camp with grandparents, aunts and uncles. They lived there for several years.

It was during the time of living in fishcamp that I was born.

That Fall the whole family moved from Fishcamp to a place across the river to "Fall" out. "Falling" out was a term used to describe living in a camp during the late fall time to hunt. At this camp, a hole was dug in the ground as foundation to built a cabin. Striped trees were used to make the sides of the house. Grass and dirt covered the sides and roof. It was sort of a sod house, but was cozy and comfortable. They lived there from about the first part of October until early December.

Across the "Fall Camp" near our fishcamp, dad left the fishwheel running late into the fall for late fish. He would get the fish and store it in a wooden box to keep frozen.

Willow grouse was plentiful at that time. Dad would hunt daily and get many of the small fowl. Mom plucked the feathers, clean the insides and stored the birds in the cache to keep frozen. The willow grouse was delicious when fried or roasted.

When it was time for my birth, my parents moved temporarily to Holy Cross to await my arrival. They traveled with my older sisters to the village by dog sled. This was in December, one of the coldest months. Dad lined the bottom of the sled with a canvas tarp and laid blankets on top for us to sit in and keep us all covered. In front of the sled under the tarp, he kept a lantern for heat. Mom said everyone was real warm snuggled under the many blankets and from the lantern heat. But because the small girls were warm mom had a hard time keeping my sisters, who were in their two and three years, sitting down quietly. The heat gave them energy and they wanted to stand and move around to play in the sled.

When reaching Holy Cross, my parents stayed in a small cabin (that is still standing at this time) in the village. The day I was born, dad was out hunting. Returning late that evening, he somehow knew he had a family member newly arrived. Rushing into the house, he left his dogs untied in the yard, so excited he was to see me. Mom said he quickly turned on the lantern and rushed to the bedside with my sisters to see me. December 19 was not far from Christmas, so he excitedly announced to the other girls that I was a Christmas present from Jesus. "See what Jesus gave us for Christmas, a little Doll Doll" he said. That's how my pet name came to be Doll Doll, which dad called me at times.

The other pet name I had was from some old folks in the village. They were close friends to dad. They named me "mump girl", since mumps was going around in the village at the time I was born. That name also stuck with me, until their death in the mid 70's. No matter when I saw them they greeted me with the same name of "mump girl". When I visited the village with my daughter in the 70's, they lovingly named her "little mump girl". What special people these older folks were. I still remember them as years go by and the memories of living and growing up with them in the village will always be special.

The kindness, self respect, respect for others they taught by their everyday lives should always be on our mind. The examples of kindness and teachings from these older folks are something we should all pass on to our children.

The one thing I always remember old folks telling us was not to talk or be noisy when an elder was talking. Also, we were never to talk back to our parents or elders. We were to have and show respect for adults always.

Another advice given to us was about food. My grandparents passed this advice to my parents that food was always to be respected. In the older days, there were many starvations where food was scarce. Animals, fowl and fish would not be enough to keep people fed throughout the winter. Starvations would happen. So the older people had respect in the treatment of food. We were never to waste food, always share with others what we have and never to step on food if on the floor.

23

Mom and dad were strict about this so even now I find myself being careful if I drop bread crumbs or other foods on the floor.

After my birth, my parents remained in the village until February 4, 1943, when they then returned to fishcamp.

Days of living in fishcamp were filled with work for survival. At the time we lived with relatives there, when I was a baby, my grandpa, dad and uncles trapped during the winter and spring, while summer days were filled with fishing activities.

During winter trapping season, furs such as martin, mink, lynx, wolverines, fox and sometimes wolves were caught. Spring brought the beaver and muskrat trapping season. Trapping was one of the important money making events for village people in those days. It wasn't done to be cruel to animals, but was important for everyday survival.

While dad was out in the trapline, mom would walk to the surrounding woods and set traps also. At one time, when checking her traps, she discovered she caught a fox but it had gotten away. When dad returned she told him about it, so he set out with his trusty gun to track the wounded fox. He caught the fox and returned to camp, and showed mom how to skin and dry the fur. When this was done, dad took it to the village to sell with his other furs. Asking mom, what special item she wanted with the money the fox would provide, she said she would like a new blanket.

At that time, mom sewed all the clothes and blankets we needed. I guess she was tired of sewing blankets, and decided she needed to buy a new one.

When we girls were babies, living in fishcamp and later in the village, mom made all our little dresses. She said she had rows of clothes lines filled with small dresses of all colors and designs that she hand sewed for us. When Spring came grandma showed mom how to make water boots for us small girls to play out in the Spring breakup water. Grandma gave mom reindeer skin and told her to scrape off the hair. After the hair was all removed, grandma showed mom some special willow bark to color the skin. The bark of the willow was stripped and put on the skin, rolled up and left overnight, leaving a reddish color on the skin. Small boots were then sewn out of the skin.

Grandma told mom to check if our feet were wet after playing in the water. Mom said a little water got into the shoes so she was told to oil around the needle holes. This stopped the leaking and made the shoes waterproof.

In fishcamp, when Christmas came, due to having no money to buy toys, mom made small cloth dolls for us. She was pretty handy with the needle. Today, she is still doing crafts, such as making dolls, mukluks, slippers, bead work and basket making. Born in 1919 her age has not slowed down her artistic skills.

Other chores keeping everyone busy in fishcamp was to go out with dog sled during winter days for wood and water. If the water creek froze, ice blocks were cut from the river, or snow was melted. Dad instructed mom to boil the water before giving us to drink, especially when there was an epidemic in the village of Holy Cross where the Catholic mission was located.

Many people in the village died from that epidemic. It was said that the mission was almost empty of children. So many people died,

Head-bands and feather wooden frame used for Native dancing.

25

graves were dug, the dead were wrapped in canvas and buried side by side in mass graves. This was because there were so many deaths people could not keep up with individual funerals and coffin making.

As I mentioned earlier, grandpa Savage was known to be a medicine man. In those days people believed in and respected medicine men/women. They relied on them for healing and good luck. The year during the epidemic in Holy Cross, grandpa told mom he would work something out to protect us. We will never know if his magic did the work or were we just lucky. The epidemic never reached our fishcamp.

At that time, people didn't want medicine men or women to be mad at them. When mom lived in her village, people relied on and believed strongly on medicine people. They made sure to share their

Miniature sled is made by dad Pius Savage Sr. modeled after sleds used in the village. Doll is made by mom Ellen Savage, modeled how Indian women dressed in her village going for winter berries when she was a child. Birch bark canoe is made by mom, modeled after canoes her dad made to ride in going hunting or berry picking. On the left is Dorothy's first birch bark basket. In reality it looks pretty rough, but this picture makes it look better than it looks.

hunting catches and other things with them to bring good luck in the future.

Mission priests sometimes made their rounds to surrounding fishcamps for Sunday mass. They set up their alter and other mass objects on the kitchen table in one of the small cabins. Everyone in camp would attend to hear the mass and receive communion. Then they shared a meal with the missionaries, who would then travel to the next camp, or back to Holy Cross.

Dad sometimes took the missionaries hunting. He told stories of the fun he had sharing stories with them about the wilderness. They would "Siwash" out, that is sleep out under pine trees, or in a tent. When living in the village, dad would hunt for the mission, sharing with them the moose, fish or geese/ducks he caught.

When my grandparents and parents lived in the fishcamp, they lived in small log cabins along the flat part below the hilly sides of our camp. This area is a little above the present location of our camp.

Dad traveled away from the camp daily by boat, to cut logs for our small cabin, until he finally had enough logs. He used the small boat to pull the logs a little at a time to fishcamp. The boat motor was about 2 or 3 horsepower. When he moved all the logs to camp, he gathered three at a time, tied them together, hooked up the dogs and had the dogs pull the logs out of the river, up the bank to the cabin area. Alone, dad worked until the cabin sides were getting too high to lift the logs. He then laid two poles to the upper side of the cabin from the ground. The log he wanted to lift was then laid at the bottom of these slanting poles, with a rope to one end. The rope was then pulled until the log reached the place it would be laid, and then tied securely. The other end of the log was then pulled up with a rope by mom and grandma until it was in place. They held on to the rope while dad tied it securely. It was sort of a pulley style process repeated until finally all logs were securely in place and the roof was ready to put on. Dad worked very hard at building the cabin, and when it was finished, it was a comfortable, place for us small children to live in.

My grandparents, aunts and uncle lived in tents also, until they built similar cabins nearby.

For several years they lived in the camp, living off the land with a subsistence life style. Hard work was a daily chore, with everyone doing their own jobs of working for survival.

It was while living in fishcamp, that World War II was heard to have started. Mom remembers several happenings in fishcamp during that time of the war. I'll share a few memories of her stories with you.

One funny story was of the local men gathering from surrounding camps and practicing marching/drilling for the national guard, in those days called the Territorial Guard, when World War II was happening. One older man was the leader who drilled and marched with the men daily. They gathered on the frozen river across our fishcamp in the fall camp and proceeded to march to his commands. Sometimes the men would get mixed up and move in different directions, not understanding him.

The old man told them the redcoats were coming and they had to be prepared to defend themselves. Old grandpa Savage sat on the bank watching and would laughingly mumble to himself that they didn't have a chance if the redcoats arrived. He said they would be wiped out.

Mom and the other women found the leader of the guards' commands and tactics funny and sat on the bank laughing and giggling over the drills. The old man ignored them and continued with his drilling, but his wife would get angry at the laughing women. He responded to their laughing by telling them they wouldn't laugh if the redcoats came.

Another story happened during World War II. I was a small baby then with three older sisters. My maternal grandmother from Shageluk was visiting at that time.

On this particular day, dad was traveling by dog sled to check his trapline and planned to be gone the whole day. As he opened the door to leave he told mom to listen to the battery operated radio he had in the house. "You might hear of something happening" was his warning to mom.

Grandpa Savage traveled away from camp by dogsled also to cut wood that day. Sometime during the day, mom said she suddenly heard a loud noise. Like a booming sound. Running outside, she and others in the camp saw a long log shaped object with fire in the end, traveling across the camp toward Aniak, Alaska. It made a loud booming sound like a gunshot and seemed like it hit the ground across in the tundra somewhere. The vibration noise sounded like loud thunder and was heard for several minutes behind the camp in the hills.

Mom was so frightened and excited by this object, she ran into the cabin and yelled at everyone there to kneel down and pray. "The end of the world is here", she told my grandma, who was sitting calmly near the window, holding me on her lap. Mom then started to dig through boxes, looking for our clothes, telling grandma we had to travel to Holy Cross right away. She ran outside, seeing grandpa coming up the bank with the dog sled loaded with wood. Running behind the sled, helping him push it up the bank, she told him to hurry, because "the Germans are coming. The war was coming to our area." Grandpa didn't seem to pay attention to her excitement and continued to push his sled calmly up the bank.

After this was all over, when she calmed down, mom discovered the house was a mess, with clothes and boxes scattered all over the small cabin. She didn't realize how frenzied she looked with her hair all a mess and her eyes as big as marbles. The excitement was just too much for her. But she finally calmed down, realizing the flying object brought no harm to them and seeing that it didn't bother the other fishcamp residents.

Grandpa found her very comical, when he laughingly described her actions of that day. He told my two grandmas that he never heard mom talk to him so much and never saw her moving around so quickly as that day. He thought she was pretty funny, running around hysterical and yelling about the end of the world and the Germans.

Listening to the radio, when dad returned from trapline, they learned that the flying object was seen by other surrounding villages. Dad had seen it also from his trapline area. He said he didn't get excited about it and was not frightened as mom was. No one seemed to know what the object was.

One year, while living in fishcamp, my aunt (dad's sister) became very ill. For days she suffered acute stomach pains. Dad finally took the dog team to the village to ask the nuns for help or medication. They did send something, probably sulpha pills, the largely used medication in those days. Sulpha pills was used to cure every ailment we were hit by.

After a few days auntie finally felt better, but grew worst again and died shortly after that. In later years, it was said she had appendicitis which could have been taken care of if correct medical care was available. At that time, medical care was not available in many of the remote villages, so people depended on their own medication or local medicine men for treatment. Women died from simple childbirth, people died from infections, pneumonia, and flu.

Older people made their own medicines out of local plants. These medicines were very effective to cure all kinds of ailments. Some of them are still used by people who know how to prepare the plants for healing remedies. I know of several people who boil a certain leafy plant to make a bitter tasting brew that is said to be a cure for some medical problems such as arthritis, colds and flu. Grandma used to boil pine tree needles to make a drink, like cough syrup.

After living in fishcamp for several years, the family all moved to Holy Cross.

It was about 5 or 6 years before we returned to our fishcamp for summer fishing. My grandparents had died by that time, so we were the only family living there. Sometimes my cousin and her family visited or stayed to fish with us.

Chapter 3

Moving to camp was always a very busy time. We brought everything but the kitchen sink, so goes the saying. Preparation and packing took days, or even months. I think we started as early as April when the snow was starting to melt.

The boat needed repair, so that was always first to do. On warm sunny Spring days you could see men throughout the village working on their boats. Right after ice breakup everyone would put their boats in the river. On clear, calm evenings dad would take us out for our first boat ride of the summer. Riding up or down the river, we could see drift wood and chunks of ice floating by. It was always exciting to have our first boat rides.

In the first year of our fishcamp moving preparations, dad made our first boat. The boat was built in the yard in front of our house. This was in the first location of our house at the end of the village. For weeks dad worked daily on building the "gas boat" as it was called in those days. Everyone had the same kind of boat, run by an old engine that was 3 or 5 horsepower. When the boat was finished, it had to be moved to the river.

The bank to the river was about a mile away from our house, reached by a path through the woods. To move the boat, dad put smooth logs under the boat, attached a long rope to the front and all of us kids pulled it. As we moved, dad would take a log from the back and move it to the front to assure we had logs under the boat to keep it rolling. One time, when moving the log, dad tripped and fell, but not knowing this we kept pulling and ran right over his leg. It's a good thing he only had an injured ankle and not a broken leg. We stopped pulling when we heard his yells for help. We all thought it was pretty funny and laughed at him,

Dad (Pius Savage Sr.) sitting in the boat he is repairing. Behind him is a wheelbarrow we used for carrying water in summer and supplies to the boat when moving to fishcamp.

until we realized he was injured. He had to be checked by the mission nun who was the local nurse. Dad was on crutches for a while, but thank goodness he didn't have any broken bones.

Another pre fishcamp preparation was making a fishnet. My parents made a net with a small wooden (knitting needle) that they made. They hung the net along the clothes line and worked on it daily for several weeks until it was completed. Heavy twine was used for the net material. When the net was completed small led like sinkers were attached along the top row. Small round wooden ball like floats were attached on the top side of the net to keep it floating when set in the river.

Moving to fishcamp took a lot of different preparations. A few days before moving we did our baking, laundry, tended our garden,stocked up with groceries, rock salt for fish strips and prayed for nice weather on travel day. It was fun preparing for the move but a lot of work. Mom did her yearly sewing of mosquito nets, and also mended clothes and socks.

Sometimes, before the final move, a boat load of supplies were taken to camp a few days before. When we had a washing machine even that went to camp.

Our first washer was a foot crank start type with a wringer on the top side, but we welcomed it at wash time. Before we had the washer we did laundry with a washboard and had to hand wring the clothes. Blisters were on our hands by the time washing was over. Later we had a clothes wringer that we had to hand turn. It was easier than wringing clothes and wearing out our hands. In fishcamp clothes were hung on the clothes lines attached from the house to the smokehouse. In the village we had a clothes line in the yard next to our house. Sun and wind dried clothes always smelled fresh and clean.

Baking was another pre fish camp move preparation. Yeast bread, baking powder biscuits were made. One year mom made a large batch of her delicious cake donuts. They were stored in our kitchen on top of the high cupboard. The busy activities of moving made everyone forget the donuts. Halfway down the river to camp mom and dad suddenly had wide eyes and a big discussion was going on between them. We couldn't hear them because of the loud boat motor noise. But we later found out they had just discovered the donuts were forgotten and still in our house on top of the cupboard. Oh well, a few weeks later when we returned to the village, for shopping and tending the garden, we found the donuts, but they were past the eating stage. What a waste.

When we lived in our old house at the end of the village, everything had to be hand or wheelbarrow carried to the river where our boat was. We made trip after trip with the wheelbarrow and the old wheel cart we had. It took us many trips to get everything moved.

After we moved to our new house above the mission, we had to carry the supplies to the bluff above the village where our boat was. Sometimes we lucked out and dad would borrow the mission truck. But we still had to load the truck at the house and unload at the boat. Then at camp we had to unload the boat again. It's no wonder I was such a skinny kid, from all that work and exercise.

On moving day it took at least half a day to load our boat. The boat seemed to be real big since it carried all our supplies, bedding, gas drum and us. We had a smaller boat we towed behind our bigger boat that was used to carry our dogs. We had about 7 to 10 dogs and they were always wild, barking loudly and anxious for the trip. We tied them in the boat to the side rafters, so they wouldn't be jumping in and out of, and everywhere and not be fighting, arguing and falling overboard.

One moving year, as we were traveling to fishcamp, we were in the middle of the river when one of the dogs came loose. He fell overboard so we had to circle and go back to pick him up. Thank goodness it was a nice day so the river was calm, except for the waves made from the boat. But the happy ending was that we rescued the dog and it seemed he settled down a little after that. I guess the cold water experience taught him a lesson.

Sometimes, as we traveled to camp, we would get caught in a wind storm and had to travel in rough waves. The rough waters seemed to be bad, but after seeing ocean waves the rough river was nothing in comparison, but still pretty scary.

During rough weather, dad traveled as close to shore as he could. The boat bounced up and down between and over the waves. It was frightening, especially since we were usually very loaded with supplies. Sometimes dad would have to cross the river with the boat in huge waves. As he expertly maneuvered the boat between the waves, I would be so scared that I would sit on or lay in the bottom of the boat and cover my head.

It's amazing how we traveled in storms and not one of us knew how to swim, and we never heard of life preservers. I always had a plan in my mind of how I would save myself if we swamped in the rough waters. I would hold on to a paddle and float to shore. Another thought I had was to have a rope to tow everyone else to shore with. Big plans, but luckily I didn't have to put my survival skills to test.

Sometimes if the weather was bad, we traveled through a slough below the village called "Fat John Slough". It took longer, but was calmer and came out to the main Yukon river about ten miles above our fishcamp. We still had to travel quite a ways on the main river but going by the slough helped some during rough weather.

I enjoyed traveling through this slough which was not too wide and had calm, clear waters. The scenery was breathtaking, quiet and serene with wildlife all around. You could see small lakes here and there in back of smaller sloughs. Ducks, loons and geese would be singing their happy summer songs. Birds would be darting in and out of the woods, over our boat and over the water. Swallows would be flying happily around us. At times the swallows would be flying dipping close to the water. Mom and dad said that was a sign of coming rain. Their simple method of weather forecast always seemed to come true. Maybe if the present weather forecasters used some of the old methods they would be a little bit more accurate.

Sometimes we would see a bear or moose if we were traveling later in the day. Traveling in the evening was my favorite time. I would sit snuggled between the bedding and clothes boxes content to watch the surrounding land and hear the wood noises and feel the smooth boat breeze on my face.

Halfway between the village and our camp we sometimes stopped for lunch. A small fire was made, a kettle was set on a wooden stake over the fire, to boil water for tea. Bread or crackers with fish were the main courses for lunch. The mosquitoes had fun eating off of us also. I liked to sit next to the smoke, as this helped keep mosquitoes and gnats away a little. Our tea and food tasted real good next to a camp fire.

Stopping for lunch was also a much needed rest stop for us small kids as we took our turns running into the woods looking for a bathroom area, fighting the mosquitoes as well. Mom and dad would call us all back into the boat and make a head count to make sure they didn't forgot anyone. We then continued our journey to fishcamp.

During some fishcamp travels, we sometimes stopped at other camps for a short visit. During these stops, we were welcomed by campers and offered a cup of tea with smoked or boiled fish, along with bread or crackers. People welcomed visitors as it gets kind of lonesome at times being in the remote camp sites for weeks.

Reaching our camp was a busy time full of work. It was great to be back after a year of being away. Dad set a plank from the boat to shore and we all used the plank to get off the boat. Running up the bank we visited the house, smokehouse and fish cutting house to see if everything would be the same as we left it. Sometimes we left things hidden in secret places and we checked to see if they were still there.

While we were doing this, mom was readying our first meal. What did we eat? At times we had tea with crackers or biscuits and spam or other canned goods. If we didn't have fish or fresh meat that was it for our meal. The canned goods from the local store were not as good as the delicious first catched fish.

After our meal was done, the boat had to be unloaded, and other settling in activities done.

The dogs were first to be unloaded because they were wild and loud, barking and jumping around with excitement in the boat. Then food had to be prepared for them. We had a half of an old oil drum used for cooking food for the dogs. Their dishes (old pots or cut gas cans) were filled with water which they happily slurped up quenching their thirst after the long and sometimes hot trip. In the evening we fed them from the pot of food we cooked for them.

We tied the dogs in the wooded area back of our house on the hilly part. During hot days they were moved closer to the river bank so they would get the breeze, keeping cooler and having less problems with mosquitoes or gnats. The reason we tied them to the area back of the house was to help keep wild animals away with their barks of excitement if an animal should try to wander into our camp.

One year, as we were sleeping, I was awaken hearing excitement going on in the front cabin. I heard mom and dad talking excitedly as they ran out the door. Then I heard shots and dad running past our house toward the hill and woods. By then we were all up and running out to see what was going on. It happened that a moose had walked by our house and ran up the hill into the woods when dad shot at it. Running up the small hill after the moose and shooting at it, dad hit the moose, but it ran into the woods about two miles before dropping.

Following the moose, dad marked the area it was in so he could return to skin and cut it to be moved to camp. He then returned to camp to get us all up and after breakfast we set out to retrieve the much welcomed moose meat. It had to be skinned, cut into small pieces and hand carried back to camp. This took us about a half a day as we all carried small pieces that wouldn't be too heavy for us young girls. Some of us used small buckets that dad filled with the meat. The moose provided a much welcome change to our daily diet of fish. The small, thin steaks fried in moose fat were delicious, and we enjoyed the hot tasty soups filled with potatoes, rice and macaroni.

Mom pressure cooked some of the meat in mason jars to be kept for later use. Some of the meat was kept in the cold water of the stream next to our camp. Dad made a small water dam and tied the meat to keep it from drifting away. He then laid heavy logs over the meat to keep it under the cold water.

Chapter 4

The first day in camp, after settling in activities were done, dad would row up shore to set the fishnet. One of us kids or mom would go with him.

To me setting the net was hard to do. It always scared me to see my parents in the boat working on the net getting it ready for setting. Sometimes the weather was bad and the river would be rough with waves. I was afraid and worried about my parents going out in rough waters to set or check the nets.

A long rope on one end of the net was used to tie it to a tree or something solid on shore. The rope was long enough to allow the net to reach the rivers' deeper part. At the far end of the net a weight of some sort had to be let into the river to hold the bottom of the net down. At the top a float (usually empty gas cans) were tied to keep the top part of the net floating. It would serve as a marker so the net would be seen by boaters and not runned over.

I recall one scary incident when my parents were setting the net. Somehow the rope attached to the anchor of the net got tangled to the rudder under the boat. As the rope twisted around the rudder pulling the back end of the boat down into the river, mom was yelling at us girls on shore to get the row boat from in front of our camp. We ran on the shore to the camp to get the row boat. We had a lot of excitement for a while trying to row the smaller boat from the fishcamp to rescue them. A couple of us girls jumped into the small row boat to try to row it up to the area to rescue our parents. Two of us grabbed the oars and started to row but one was rowing frontwards and the other rowed backwards so the boat was turning in circles. It must have been a funny sight to watch, but at the time we were all so excited we didn't see the humor of it all, until later.

During all the excitement, dad, who was a fast thinker got a good idea. He quickly tied his knife to the end of a long pole (it might have been a paddle) and bent over the boat side reaching the paddle into the water under the boat and cut the rope. The boat was released and all was well, but that was a close call. Of course, no one in the boat had life jackets and they didn't know how to swim.

When checking the net for fish, dad would let one of us sit on the back of the boat and use an oar to keep the boat straight as he pulled the net over the front end. That was one of the fun parts of fishing I liked to do.

Some mornings I would wake to hear my parents already up and fixing coffee and breakfast. Dad was preparing to check the net. Laying in bed, I listened and debated on whether I should go with him or not but could not make up my mind. Finally as he was walking down to the boat I jumped out of bed, at the last minute, slipped my shoes on and ran down the bank jumping in the boat as he was shoving off. It's a good thing I slept with my clothes on or I would probably "miss my boat" many times.

While the net setting was going on, the rest of us in camp would continue getting settled in. It was a beehive of activity but didn't take long because everyone helped. The house had to be cleaned as it was a mess from the winter. Leaves, dust, tree branches, mouse droppings always were things that had to be removed. We had to put away all our supplies, claim our bed area and make our beds. Mosquito nets went up over beds throughout the room. There were so many beds in rows, it looked like a soldier's bunk house.

My recollection of the first summer we moved to fishcamp, was seeing this empty bleak place with falling logs that were once cabins and fish cutting houses. Lots of tall grass everywhere. We lived in a tent that first summer until dad renovated one of the cabins for our living quarters.

It was fun living in the tent, except on rainy days, when everything was wet or damp. But lying in bed and listening to the raindrops hit the top of the tent gave me a peaceful relaxing feeling that would put me to sleep. I liked the fresh grassy smell inside the tent too.

The tent was small so we slept side by side on the ground in our bedding. In the morning we had to roll up our bedding and pile them on top of each other in a corner. This was to make room for us to move around in the tent during the day. On sunny days we hung the bedding outside to air or dry the dampness out. There would be mattresses and blankets everywhere.

Most of the time, weather permitting, our meals were cooked outside on a makeshift stove in the yard. It was fun cooking outdoors. You could catch the delicious aroma of frying fish everywhere. We had to fight the mosquitoes and later the gnats while cooking, but the cooking smoke would help keep the little pests away.

There was the remains of a small fish cutting house that my grandparents used when they lived there in previous years for fish cutting. There were four corner poles still standing. Dad decided to rebuilt it into living quarters, so the day after we moved to camp, up went the falling logs for the frame, and the sides were covered with lumber. Dad put a tarp over the small house while working on it to keep the rain out. I remember as he was working, the weather was real bad, cold, windy and rainy, but us kids were everywhere in and out of the small building. We didn't pay too much attention to the bad weather, as we were busy and excited about setting up camp and watching dad build our new summer home. Everything our parents did was a new and exciting adventure to us.

The small house was roughly built, but it worked for the summer. I wouldn't want to live in it during the winter though. The stove used in the main house was fed with wood. It was a small Yukon stove, until from somewhere, we acquired a bigger cast iron stove with a larger oven.

Cupboards, which were wooden gas boxes, were installed on the walls. These boxes came in handy as cupboards to store dishes and were also used to store clothes in. If we had extras they were used for chairs along with a few small wood blocks.

The table was small, made from left over lumber, so most of us ate where we found a sitting place. Sometimes we sat outdoors if the mosquitoes and gnats permitted it. Of course the weather had a lot to do with that too.

The door to the house was a small wooden contraption, tied with string at night, to keep intruders out. I don't know what kind of intruders we were afraid of, probably wild animals, as people were pretty harmless in those days. Anyway the house was crude with thin walls, but workable for the summer. There was a small window on each side of the door facing the river. Outside the door, under one of the small windows, was a wooden stand used to keep our wash basin.

The house was close to the creek so we dumped our garbage and water over the side. It got pretty messy until high-water carried all that away. What a mess it got to be but no one seemed to know that was not the place to have trash. Nothing to worry about since we all didn't seem to know any better.

Added to the back of the house was another building made out of the same material but a little bigger. This part was sleeping quarters for us many kids. We had wooden beds lined in a row and protected with mosquito netting. The netting also served like a private room for us. Mom labored many hours before moving to fishcamp to sew the nets for every one of us many kids.

In the back room (the sleeping quarters) we had one window and a stove made out of an oil drum. This stove was mainly for heat. It was comforting to sit by the stove on cold rainy days reading or telling stories.

The floor in the sleeping quarters was dirt. Pieces of old lumber were laid on the ground between the beds for walking on. In the front main house we had a wooden floor. I liked the dirt floor because it didn't have to be swept, or scrubbed. Scrubbing floors with the floor brush and soap was no fun, especially to our knees.

Our first days in the fishcamp were used to repair the smoke house and preparing the fish racks in anticipation for the coming fish. It was great when the net was checked and a salmon or two was caught. We had delicious salmon steaks cooked outdoors, with side dishes of macaroni or rice, crackers or baking powder biscuits, washed down with tea. Tea was always our main meal time drink. It seems like we had tea with all our meals, including our bed time snack of crackers or biscuits.

Chapter 5

It seemed like no time at all when the fish runs began. There were about two or three runs of salmon. During those times the net was checked three times a day with a catch of anywhere from five to ten salmons, more or less. Mom was the fish cutter making salmon strips, flats, stomach parts, tails and heads. Salmon heads were open and split with the eyes hanging out. The eyes, when dried and smoked, were delicious for eating. Sometimes we sneaked into the smokehouse and picked eyes out of the smoked and dried salmon heads to chew on. Yum, yum. Our mouths would get black and that's how our parents knew we were into the salmon eyes. Sometimes they would wonder out loud about what happened to all the salmon eyes on the fishheads in the smokehouse.

Another thing we did was to insert dog fish heads into a long pole until it was full. We would then hang the head poles on the outside fish rack to dry. The heads were used for dog food during the winter.

The first years in fishcamp we kids were younger and didn't know much about fish cutting. When small white fish were caught in the fishwheel, mom let us scrape the scales off the sides and open the stomach and clean out the fish. She gave us the small fish telling us to work at cutting the fish on the grassy parts of the yard. Here we would sit, laboring over the small fish trying to remove all the scales before cutting to hang for smoking. This was one way of learning how to cut and care for fish. Later on when we were older we had to help with cutting the dog fish caught in the fishwheel.

When the fishwheel was used we had a lot of "dog fish" to cut. During heavy fish runs, the fishwheel box would be full and had to be checked about three times a day. We had a long wooden table dad built for cutting. The table had holes here and there, with empty gas cans or

43

plastic buckets under, for throwing fish "guts" and unused fish heads into. When the containers were full, they were stacked one side of the fish house. When all the containers were full, we loaded them unto the boat and took them to the middle of the river to dump. Sometimes the guts were buried in deep holes in the back of our smokehouse. Mostly we dumped them in the river. Less flies and worms resulted from the latter.

During heavy fish runs, it seemed like we were busy cutting fish all day. The fishwheel was checked in the morning, after lunch and before supper. Sometimes we even checked it in the evening. When checking the fishwheel, we tied the boat next to the basket and using a long pole with a hook at the end would empty the box of fish to the tubs in the boat. Fish caught had to be cut right away and hung out to dry. We didn't have coolers or ice to keep them from spoiling in the hot sunny days.

When cutting fish, one of my favorite things to do was to save fish hearts. I had a container by me, used to save the small hearts for my lunch. They were quite delicious, when fried with onions, or sometimes just plain boiled. At times we would boil fish hearts and eggs together for lunch.

We formed sort of an assembly line cutting the fish. The first person would cut the head off and open the stomach. That was usually me, so I could save the hearts. The next person would clean the stomach out. Then on down the line someone would flat the fish, usually mom. A narrow piece of wood was inserted across the middle of the flat fish to keep it from folding when hanging to dry.

The knives we used to cut the fish were called "Indian knives", better known as ulus. Dad was an expert at making these knives.

The narrow wooden sticks, used to hold the flatted fish open, were made by dad, out of dry wood blocks. The wood blocks were hand split into narrow kindling like sticks. These were tied together in bundles and saved to use when we had a lot of dog fish to cut. As we were cutting fish, dad would sit next to our cutting table and make the wooden sticks. He would also keep the small fires going around our fish cutting table to

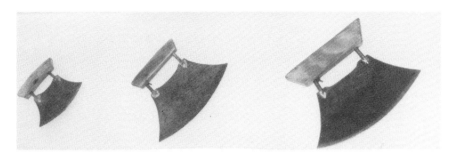

Indian knives dad made for fishcutting. Used to slice moose and fowl also. Great for slicing onions and pancakes.

make smoke for keeping mosquitoes and gnats away. Some evenings, he would sit on the bank and split the wood for these small fish sticks.

When the cutting was complete we threw the fish in a wheelbarrow near the table. The loaded wheelbarrow was then taken to the fish rack to hang and be sun dried along with smoke. The sun drying was only done to the "dog fish". This process took about a week or so. When the fish was half dried, they were moved to the smoke house for the final smoke drying process.

We had a small four sided wooden box along the shore that dad made to throw the fish into. Next to it was the cutting table to clean and cut the fish. We had a long narrow pole with a hook, made out of a bent nail at the end of it, to hook the fish and throw them into the wooden box. This hook was the same one used at the fishwheel, to load the fish from the fishwheel box to the containers (usually old tubs) in the boat.

During the heavy dog fish runs, the fishcutting table was moved under the bank next to the river. This was because there was so much fish it helped, that we could unload the fish from the boat right to the four sided box next to shore. Tree branches were put in the bottom of the box to keep the fish from getting sand or mud on them.

On hot days, dad made a shade out of canvas tarps, around the cutting table to protect us from the hot summer sun. At times it got so hot we could hardly stand it and cutting the fish made the heat seem worse.

One day as we were cutting fish, my sister started to act a little strange and looked pale, as if she was about to faint. Mom got so excited she grabbed a bucket of water kept nearby that we used for washing our hands. She dipped her hand in the slimy, bloody water and washed my sister's face. That revived her fast and her fainting spell was over. I don't know if the cold water helped, or maybe the smelly, slimy water acted as ammonia to revive her. Anyway she was sent to bed and her fish cutting was done for that day.

The smokehouse was made out of logs standing on four corners and covered on top with tin sheets. The sides were covered with old lumber mixed with tin sheets. When we first moved to camp we didn't have enough material to cover the sides of the smokehouse, so a makeshift wall was made out of tree poles and leaves. The poles were made into a frame and tied crisscross with roots. Leave branches were piled on top of this to cover the whole frame. Another pole frame was laid on top and tied to the bottom frame. Sort of a leaf sandwich. This was lifted to the side of the smoke house and tied together to make a wall. What an interesting wall. I thought dad was pretty smart to make a wall out of the forest. Each year after that he somehow got enough material to cover the sides of the smokehouse so eventually we didn't have to use the branch wall.

On the ground, in the smokehouse, there were four holes for keeping fire going to smoke the fish. Fire had to be kept going day and night, everyday until the drying process was done. This usually took about two to three weeks. The fire holes were about two and a half feet wide, about four feet long and a foot and a half deep.

The wood used in the smokehouse had to be dry wood. Wet wood, or green wood as it was sometimes called, we were told would make the fish sour and moldy.

Getting the wood was a job the whole family did. We took the boat up or down river and stopped where we saw a lot of drift wood on shore along the river banks. Mosquitoes and gnats didn't seem to bother us, although they were aplenty. Wood gathering was another job I enjoyed doing. After filling the boat with wood, we returned to camp and unloaded them into a pile next to the smoke house. This was done several times a week to ensure not running out of wood in case the weather didn't allow us to go out some days.

The wood then had to be cut to size. We had a saw horse, made of logs, forming an x on each side and held together in the middle with a single log nailed at each end. We laid the wood to be cut on top of this and used a long narrow saw with a handle on each end. It took two of us girls to do the wood cutting. It was hard sawing, but it was easier if two of us did the job. Then we had to use the axe and split the blocks to smaller sized pieces for firewood. For smoke house use, we cut the logs to smaller pieces with the saw, but thank goodness we didn't have to chop them.

When we had whole logs with the root like ends, we would place the whole end in the smokehouse fire hole to burn slowly thus making smoke longer.

Moving the fish to the smokehouse was another process. The smoke house as I mentioned before, was a small building with about three racks (one on top of the other). The building was small, about twenty to twenty five feet in diameter. When hanging fish we started at the top rack until that rack was full. We then moved to the next rack on down until all racks were full.

Hanging fish in the smokehouse was quite an experience. I was usually chosen to climb up to the third tier to hang the salmon strips. The fish was oily and drippy and I had to sit between all that, on an oily plank. Wow what a smell. I wonder how I smelled after finishing with that job. No jumping into the shower for me though. I don't think I even gave it a thought. Washed my face and hands and that was that.

But I didn't worry about the smell or the dripping oil and continued hanging the fish until all was done.

During the summer months, when the fish was in the smokehouse for a while, we would start checking the first dried ones to see if they were ready for eating. It was great to eat the first dried fish. After the long hard work of the summer, getting the fish smoked it was a reward when it was finally ready for eating.

King salmon were caught in the fishnet, mostly. Once in a while a stray would be in the fishwheel. After taking the salmon from the nets, we returned to camp, hauling the fish up the bank with a wheelbarrow. Mom would have breakfast ready and right after eating, would start cutting the salmon. She had a different area for cutting salmon. It was a small partly open sided, closed topped building, which had about two small holes in the ground for smoking the cut fish.

When first cut, the salmon was kept hanging to dry in the cutting house. Smoke was kept going during the day under the fish. About a week or so later the fish would be moved into the covered smokehouse for full smoking. Salmon eggs were dried and smoked. When dried they tasted pretty good, but were a little sticky and left an after taste in our mouth.

A salt brine was made to dip the strips in. I think the fish was left in the brine about three to four minutes. Then the strips were hung inside the building and smoked for a couple of weeks. The next step was to move the strips into the closed in smokehouse. This was done in the same way as the other fish. Lots of dripping oil and strong fish smell was in the smoke house. Strips, flats, stomach parts were cut and flatted for hanging to smoke.

Another way to store fish was to salt it. Using a small barrel, rock salt was lined on the bottom, then a slab of salmon was laid on top. The process of rock salt, alternating with a salmon slab was continued until the barrel was full. The barrel was then covered and sealed, ready for use during winter months.

When the salt fish was ready for use, we had to soak it for a day before cooking. Boiled or baked it tasted pretty good, just like fresh salmon.

Half dried fish was also eaten. The fish hanging to dry was used before it was fully dried. We boiled the half dried fish for about fifteen minutes before eating. This was called "Ginavagh". Half dried split salmon tails and heads were a favorite when cooked.

Pressure cooked salmon in jars was another way to store fish. The fish were put in mason jars with salt, pepper, onions and a little water.

The jar was then covered with a rubber gasket, the lid was put on and closed. The jars, about five or six, depending on the size of the cooker, were put into the pot on the stove. The pressurized cooking was done for about fifteen to twenty minutes. It's been many years, so I'm guessing on the time. After the cooking time was up, the steam was released from the pot. The hot steamy jars were then removed and let to cool before storing in cases.

In fish camp when we caught fish, we sometimes saved the eggs for eating. Salmon eggs would be dried and smoked. These were delicious and "rich" in taste. The small, bead like eggs from white fish were sometimes eaten raw. Mixed with chopped onions, salt and pepper they made a delicious caviar. This mixture was called "bussock" by the native people at that time.

When my grandparents lived in camp they prepared fish caviar by digging large deep holes in the ground. These holes were then lined with birch bark. Fishheads or eggs were put into the birch bark lined holes, covered securely, and left to ferment for several weeks. Finally when the food was done fermenting, it would be removed and eaten. This preparation had to be done carefully so no air would get to the food. If that happened danger from food poisoning was always a worry. Dad and mom said the food was very good. But that sort of food didn't sound good and didn't appeal to my taste buds.

Another native way of eating fish was to eat it raw, frozen. During winter, dad would keep white fish in a sack on top of the porch to keep it frozen. Every once in a while, he would slice pieces out of the frozen fish for eating. He sometimes shared it with us, but mom didn't want us eating the frozen raw fish. She was always afraid we would get a stomach ache from it.

Her treatment of stomach aches in those days was to give us caster oil. What a bad tasting medicine that was. Sometime she would give us this other bad tasting stuff called cod liver oil for vitamins. It tasted so bad, I would sometimes spit it out. We were a little stubborn to take the oils, so mom would offer us a spoon of sugar to take away the bad taste.

Chapter 6

The first year we moved to fishcamp, dad had to make a new fishwheel. Several long logs were gathered and tied together for the raft, about three or four logs side by side on each four sides of the wheel. In the middle of the raft, a frame was built to hold the two large baskets that turned around and around, pushed by the river current making the wheel turn, dipping into the river. Fish were caught and slide by the chute located in the center of the two baskets, into a box on the side of the wheel raft. At the end of the wheel, on the raft, there was one long pole used for stopping the wheel from turning. One of us would hold on to the basket, as it came out of the water while dad would insert the log on the opposite side basket to stop it.

One summer, in an area located across our fishcamp, there was a huge forest fire. The fire was located in a slough far back in the tundra. Boats were used to reach the site, and many of the village men and boys were hired to fight the fire. Dad, uncle and my older cousins were some of the fire fighters, so only mom and us kids were left to take care of the fishing. My aunt (mom's sister) and her children stayed with us. She wasn't much help, as she was scared out of her wits by any noises, dogs barking and was also scared of boating. Poor woman almost drove mom crazy with her worry about wild animals and other forest creature noises.

When we were checking the fishwheel with the boat at one time, the engine exhaust pipe was jolted loose. The loud noise was sudden and surprised us all. Auntie jumped up in the boat and ran fast forward, stopping when she realized she had no place to run. That incident was one of the funny stories we shared for months, even years after. Mom calmly reconnected the exhaust pipe and continued driving the boat without any excitement to her.

Finally, due to the strange noises auntie was always hearing, we moved to the upper fishcamp. A tent was pitched on the shore in front of the camp, where we stayed until the men returned from fire fighting. During days, we traveled to our camp to feed the dogs and check fires in the smoke house, check nets, the fishwheel, and cut daily caught fish.

When dad returned from fire fighting, it was almost time to move back to the village. He had quite a lot of money, (we thought back then). I think he had about $1000. That was when he bought mom her first washing machine. Gone were the days of scrubbing clothes with the washboard. A job that usually took several days, especially in fishcamp. We had six small boys to keep clean so wash days usually lasted about two or three days. We had long clothes lines used to hang diapers and clothes to dry.

One day in fishcamp, the rinse water in the washtub came in handy. On this particular day, I got up early, and went outside to wash my face. As I walked toward the smokehouse to check my bird traps, I noticed flames, that I could see through the many holes in the side of the walls. Opening the door, I saw huge flames reaching up toward the hanging fish. I quickly returned to the house and calmly told my parents that I thought the smoke house might be on fire. I tried to be calm because I didn't want to excite my parents. But when they heard my calm report, they jumped up and ran quickly to the smoke house. Following closely behind mom, her and I grabbed the clothes tub filled with water, and continued running to the smokehouse. Dumping the water on flames, we quickly put the fires out. That was a close call. After that dad made sure to check the tin sheets laid over the fire holes to make sure they were not covered with oil. The fish oil was always a danger for fire starting.

On rainy days we spent our time in the house or smoke house. In the house we sat by the stove and read or talked and told stories. I loved to read but reading material was limited.

Sometimes we played cards with our parents. Rummy was the biggest game in our card life. Chinese Checkers was another game we liked to play. We didn't mind if we lost our cards or other things, but we guarded our Chinese checkers carefully. It was fun to pull out the checkers on a rainy day or in the evening and play for hours.

On sunny days we had more fun. We went boating to the many sloughs surrounding the fishcamp area. On Sunday's we went on picnics and berry picking trips, when the salmon berries were ready. Sometimes we went hunting with our parents.

We played in the water right above our fishcamp on a small lagoon like inlet. The water in this area was shallow and still, just right for playing in. We didn't know how to swim, so mostly we ran around splashing and cooling off. Sometimes, our parents took us with the boat to a small sandbar located across the camp. The water was shallow so we were able to enjoy playing and running around in it. We were always cautioned by our parents not to go too far out in the river water.

While we were playing around, our parents would walk to the willow area to look for willow roots. Sometimes we helped them pull the roots out of the ground. The roots had to be found in the sand and pulled out. Sometimes they were quite long and hard to pull but we got the job done. Mom took the roots back to camp where she and dad stripped away the outer shell of the roots then split them. These would be dyed with dye purchased from the store. Then she would make a willow root tray or birch basket for selling.

None of us kids learned to do baskets at that time. Early in the 1980's I learned to do birch basket making while living in Anchorage. Mom had given me a basket and looking at it I finally figured out how to do the craft.

Splitting the roots was a trick to do. I never learned to do that for a while, until my husband, Angus Joseph from the village of Beaver, Alaska, figured out the trick of splitting roots and showed me how to do that. It got quite easy to do after several practices. With his encouragement and helpful ideas, my root splitting and basket making improved after several years.

I learned to design different shapes and sizes of baskets, pin cushions, tree ornaments, thread spool holders and birch bark earrings. My three children all had their try at basket making. They did real good and when they were younger children, seemed to enjoy the craft. My daughter in-law, with my help has made several baskets also.

Recently I accomplished the art of sewing Indian summer cloth parkys. Mom was getting ready for a parky feast potlatch in the village in honor of deceased relatives. She chose several people to portray, dad, grandfathers, grandmothers, uncle and brother. Mom cut out the cloth for the two parkys she would present to the women portraying my grandmothers. She asked me to sew the parkys, so I did. This was the first try I had at sewing parkys, but looking at the old ones I had, I guessed at how it should be done. When finished, the items looked pretty good.

I didn't know how to do the hoods, so turned those over for mom to finish. Later on I decided to try a few for myself. I used my old parkys' as patterns. Cutting out the cloth was a little tricky, trying to make designs match. When it came to the hood part, I had to try to figure out how to do that. Studying the other old parky I had, I did the job. The next few parkys I made turned out a lot better than my first. Actually, my first was not bad, just needed a little improvement on the hood part. But I

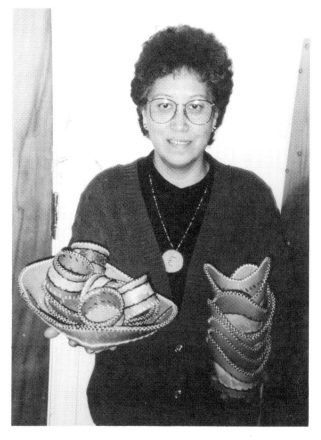

Birch baskets made by Dorothy Joseph.

succeeded, and that was the important part. I found that sewing the parkys was fun, especially picking out the cloth, matching trims and finally finishing the garments.

Indian summer parkys made by Dorothy.

Chapter 7

Getting back to fishcamp entertainment. Some evenings we all got out and played games such as hide and seek, red rover, tag, hopscotch or marbles. Tag was played under the bank on the beach. The games were fun and sometimes we got pretty noisy. Our parents called us in when things got too noisy or if it was getting late or sometimes when fights and arguments started breaking out among us kids. Everyone was tired and sweaty and ready for rest after a long day of fish cutting and games. We snacked on tea and crackers before bedtime. In our beds, before falling asleep, we read comic books or other books the mission sisters let us have for the summer. Sometimes we talked or shared stories and dreamed about returning to the village.

We also listened to music on the battery operated radio that dad set up. He would turn the radio on, probably to quiet us, and I think that worked. We all listened for our favorite songs, and sometimes would listen to news. Nome had a radio station that had a request program on every afternoon. We were sure to tune in for that everyday, as it was everyone's favorite station to listen to.

When we were younger we had "playhouses" with old tins and plates as pots, pans and dishes. Leaves, pebbles and other forest objects were used to make pretend vegetable salads. A mixture of mud and water was put on pieces of tree bark to bake in the sun for cakes and cookies.

One year when we were moving back to the village, I thought I would be real smart and store my household goods in the sand under the bank. The next year when we returned I couldn't find anything. I guess the river currents carried everything away when the water was higher over the bank. I did that with my grandmothers Indian knife. People call those knives ulus, but we called them Indian knives. Anyway, I wanted to keep it so my sisters would not take it away from me. I treasured this knife, because mom gave it to me to use when learning to cut fish. She told me it belonged to my grandmother. So I buried the knife in the sand under the bank. The next Spring, when we returned to camp, I looked for it without luck. The river currents had carried it away or the sand buried it deeper.

Other evening or daytime activities for entertainment were taking walks up the shore from our camp. Along the bank was a small path that led a little further up where old buildings were, old smoke houses and cutting houses. There was an older cabin left over from days of grandparents living there. Our relatives who visited or chose to spend the summer fishing with us would live at this site.

A little further up from there was our "cranberry garden" in the woods. When the berries were ready dad and mom would take us there to pick berries. There was such an abundance of cranberries. I would take a handful from one bunch and would fill my berry container fast. With the picked berries, mom made cases of cranberry jam for winter use.

This brings to mind the times we traveled on the river, looking for dry wood for the smokehouse or just riding, and stopping by a hillside. My parents would get out of the boat and looking under the trees where plants and ferns grew, they would find wild rhubarb. These were picked and returning to camp mom made jam or rhubarb fruit, which tasted real good with baking powder biscuits washed down with our much used "cup of tea".

Mom said when living with my grandparents in the fishcamp, grandma would pick some of the small fern leaves. She cleaned the dry parts out of the stems, washed the plants and when cooked turned out a delicious vegetable dish. Another vegetable that was fixed was wild rhubarb leaves cooked with white fish liver. This turned out to be a spinach like vegetable.

Returning to more of fishcamp entertainment. Some evenings we walked further up around the hill on the shore. We didn't go too far as there were many rocks that made it hard to walk on in that area. We usually walked as far as where the fishwheel was located. When the river water was not too high there was a nice shore to walk on.

On the lower part of fishcamp, across the small creek, where the other hill was, there was a steeper part with many large and small rocks. This was where we spend time sometimes, sitting on the larger rocks, finding flat stones to skip into the river. We would have contests to see whose rocks skipped the most and further.

As we grew older we lost interest in playhouses and things like that, and took more interest in self grooming.

Dad had a small steam bath hut made out of bent willows for the frame. A small hole was dug in the ground and the top was filled with large rocks. The hole served as a stove to make the fire to heat the rocks. When the rocks were hot, the top of the hut was covered with canvas. Water was thrown on the rocks and there was our steam bath. We used grass or branches to beat our backs to clean ourselves when the steam made us sweat. This was a great way of bathing.

Another way of entertainment and pass time in fishcamp was to catch birds. We made a trap out of pieces of skinny boards nailed together with four sides, into a frame. The flat frame was covered with wire netting, left over from use for making the fishwheel baskets. This trap was set on the ground in the back of the smoke house where birds looked for worms. A piece of wood was used to hold the front of the trap up off the ground. String, long enough to reach the smoke house, was tied to the wood holding the trap up. We sat in the smokehouse holding the string, hiding and waiting for the first victim. We put a handful of worms under the middle of the trap. It didn't take long for the birds to fall for that. When a bird walked under the trap to the middle area we pulled the string and there, we had our catch. We would be so excited, running out of the smokehouse to the back where our trap was. Reaching under the trap, we would remove the bird to a small cage we built.

At times I collected quite a lot of birds, but not as much as my sister. She collected over twenty at one time. Robin red breasts were a treat to catch because they were a little smarter than other birds and prettier. The chickadees were easy to get. We kept the birds in a small cage we made, but sometimes let them out in our bed which was covered by mosquito netting. What noisy creatures. When mom found out how many birds we had she would make us let them go. Eventually we did set them free, but continued hunting for more. This was an all summer hunting activity for us. The birds didn't seem to learn their lesson because at times I think we caught the same birds we let fly away earlier.

My last year in fishcamp was in the summer of 1962. That year we had high-water during most of the summer. The river water was over the bank, not far from our house and smokehouse. We tied our boats in front of the smokehouse. The salmon cutting house was in the water all that summer. All our fishcutting activities had to be one in the small yard right in front of the house.

The water was so high all summer even over banks into the woods. I'm sure many animals drowned from tiredness of swimming looking for ground. An example was one evening as we were out boat riding, we spotted a moose swimming across the wide river. He was swimming and looked as if he was real tired but had a long way to go to reach the other side of the river. We watched as he swam across the river but on shore where he was headed the river water was over the banks. We all wondered if the moose made it to safety somewhere.

One evening in camp, as we were sitting around the yard, someone spotted muskrats swimming close to shore. One was close to the boat, so excitedly, I ran into the boat, grabbed a paddle and started beating on the muskrat. I was so intent on getting the small animal I didn't stop to think how hard I was hitting it. Everyone was shouting at me to stop, and when I finally did, the small muskrat floated dead to the surface. I pulled it out of the water and got ready to skin the fur and dry it. While skinning the muskrat, I noted that almost every bone in his small body was broken. I felt sorry then for hitting it so long and hard. I saved the dry fur until we returned to the village, where I sold it to the local storekeeper for $1.00.

Other muskrats were swimming around in the small creek next to our house. My brother-in-law started shooting at them, with no hit. Finally, one of my younger brothers Pat, took the gun, aimed, and with one shot, downed the small furry creature. We all congratulated him on his expertness with the gun.

There was a store owner in Koyukuk, Alaska a village way up the River from Holy Cross, who traveled down the river by boat each summer with a supply barge, to trade for fish. He visited our fishcamp in late July or early August. Sometimes we were already moved to the village when he arrived.

My parents sold bundles of the "dog fish" and salmon strips to him in exchange for food and cash. We had fun shopping in the floating grocery/supply store. He had fresh fruit, such as bananas, apples, oranges and grapes, which was a welcome change to our simple diet and taste buds, especially if we were in fishcamp. The different food bought in his store was always great to have. With the extra money they received, our parents would take out the sears catalog and order shoes for us and sometimes a new set of clothes, if there was enough money.

These various activities kept us busy all summer. Days moved by swiftly and soon it was berry picking time.

In our fishcamp, we sometimes climbed the hill next to the water stream to check for salmon or early blueberries. The hill was kind of steep and took about fifteen to twenty minutes to climb. Climbing up the hill, we followed old trails made by my grandparents when they lived there. I liked climbing that mountain, walking on the trails my grandparents walked on. It made me feel close to them and I would imagine seeing them walking up that hill talking and calling to each other in their Native language.

The top of the hill was flat and mossy with a lot of berry bushes. Walking closer to the edge on the river side, we could see for miles around across and beyond the Yukon river. The scenery was breathtaking, with the stillness of the country reaching inside of us giving us the peaceful feeling of the outdoors. But we always had to stay close together because there were lots of "bear" signs. Dad would again be carrying his gun reminding us to stay close to him and not wonder off.

Salmon berry picking, usually took place during the middle of July. We traveled from our fishcamp and spent about three days camping out in the surrounding sloughs. One favorite picking area was below and across from our fishcamp. It was located in this slough, but I would never be able to find it. It's too bad we didn't think of drawing a map at that time.

It seemed like we traveled for a long time winding deeper and deeper into the slough. There were many outlets into lakes and streams. The scenery was so beautiful and quite, except for ducks and geese calling messages to each other. Loons and frogs gave us their summer songs continuously. Mountain birds could be heard crying their welcome to us, or maybe telling us to go away. A light soothing breeze always seemed to be present in the berry picking flats. The silence of the tundra would make the bird calls and the breeze seem like a loud whisper, mixed in with mosquito noises.

Just when we were getting tired of sitting in the boat traveling all day, dad finally landed the boat by a hillside. He would tie the boat to a tree branch and climb up the bank to "check" the area out. If berry signs looked good, we would set up camp there. Usually the campsite was located where the berries were. This particular place we traveled to pick salmon berries was all tundra. The moss was everywhere with a few trees or branches.

Our tent or sometimes two tents were put up and a meal of duck soup or boiled fish with macaroni or potatoes was prepared. Activities of settling in took place, while dad walked back farther to "check out" the berry situation. When he returned we had our meal and if it wasn't too late in the evening we all set out to start picking the berries close to our camp site.

While we were picking berries, Dad carried his gun and checked the area carefully for wild animals. He walked further back and sometimes called mom to follow him with us if the berries were thicker.

When the berry season was good you could see the yellow orange salmon berry color for a long ways. Usually the berries grew better near a water hole or small lakes located in areas on the tundra. I would sit in one spot and start picking and sometimes never moved far from that area because of the abundance of berries. When my container was full I emptied it into another larger container (a tub or barrel). We filled many tubs and barrels before the picking was finished. Usually we stayed for two to three days and picked all day. It got tiresome sometimes and fighting mosquitoes and gnats was no fun.

Returning to fishcamp from salmon berry picking trips seemed like we were gone forever and we were always happy to be back. Our dogs welcomed us with their barks of excitement and sounded so happy. Our first job to do when returning was to replenish the dog pots with water and start up a fire under their cooking pot to fix their meal. Of course, before leaving camp, we left enough food and water with them to last until we returned.

The salmon berries had leaves on them that had to be removed individually before storing. Usually canvas, like tarp, or blankets were spread on the ground and the berries were spread on top. The sun took care of opening the leaves which made it easier to remove them. We sat here and there around the yard and removed the tiny leaves all day, occasionally popping a berry in our mouth. It took our family about two days to take care of this boring and tedious leaf removing job. After we removed all the leaves from the berries, a sugar syrup was made to pour into a barrel to store the berries in. When filled, the barrel lid was sealed with wax and stored in a cool place until moving back to the village. In the village the barrels were stored in the cache. At the end of the fishing and berry season, our "Cache" would be filled to the door and ceiling with food for the winter. The small cellar in the house in the village kept the cases of fish, meat and berry jams safe and cool.

One year when returning to fishcamp, after a berry picking trip, we found a crow "raven" laying injured on shore. We adopted him and named him Raymond. We took it for granted it was a "he". Raymond stayed with us for a while recovering from his injuries. I don't remember what kind of injury he had but he was a fine bird that we all got attached to. At first we tied him to a pole in the yard. He was fed on fish and fish intestines which he loved and ate greedily out of our hands.

After several weeks of caring for and feeding Raymond, he recovered, but we kept him tied so he wouldn't fly away. At the end of the summer it was time to let him go. He was untied but hung around the camp anyway. He sometimes would fly off but always returned. When he flew away we would call him by name and he would return landing on our shoulder. What a thrill it was when this happened. I felt like he was our special friend. This went on for sometime and then one day he flew off and didn't return. Each year when I saw crows flying around I often wondered if one of them was our special friend "Raymond".

This brings to mind a story our parents told us when we were small children. I guess these were bedtime stories in place of "Snow White, Cinderella, etc". When my own children were small, I would tell them these stories as I remembered them, with a little spice added here and there and sang them the songs I knew.

There was this fox walking in the forest. He walked so far and long that he got real thirsty. The fox came to a lake and drank, and drank until the whole lake was empty. Of course with all the water in him he was so full he couldn't walk. He laid down and was very cold. A crow came by and the fox asked him to build a fire because the fox was so cold. The crow did and the fox laid by the fire, cold and lonely. He wiggled closer to the fire and sang "Wah, Wah, Wah, Wah, Wah, Wah, Wah, Wah. Each time he sang this tune, he wriggled closer and closer to the fire to get warm. Finally he wriggled so close to the fire, his stomach burst, and the whole lake of water he drank, gushed out and the lake was there again. The fox was so happy, he got up and ran off thanking the crow for his help.

This and many fable stories were shared with us by our parents who learned the stories from their parents.

Chapter 8

It seemed like in no time the end of summer drew near. Fish was all dried and smoked, ready for storing. This was a busy time for everyone. We had to bundle the "chum" or as we called them "dog fish". Bundling the dog fish was done so much year after year that I still remember there were "fifty" fish to a bundle.

To bundle the fish dad made a bundling rack near the smokehouse. It had three small poles hammered into the ground in a row of three, on each side about a foot apart. On the bottom of the device we laid boards to keep the fish off the ground. On the side of the smoke house, about a foot off the ground, there was a plank nailed to the wall. This was used to insert thick poles under and push down over the fish to smash the fish down and make a neat bundle. Ropes were used to tie the bundle together. Before placing fish on the rack, three ropes were laid on the bottom, so when we piled fifty of the fish on top, we mashed them down and reached under for the ropes and while several of us sat on the poles holding the fish down one of us would be in charge of tying the knots. The bundles were heavy so it took two of us girls to lift and carry them to store in the smoke house until moving day.

Bundling fish sometimes took us two to three days of all day work. The sticks used to hold the flat fish open had to be broken and removed. Then we fold the fish in half the long way to put in the bundle. What a tedious, oily and smelly job. When we were finished for the day there was a pile of broken sticks on the ground. We gathered them to save and use for kindling to start fire in the wood stove or smoke house.

The salmon strips had to be prepared for moving also. If we had cans we did the canning in fishcamp, but most of the time this job was saved until we moved back to the village. The strips were removed from the hanging poles in the smoke house. We tied a bundle of them together and wrapped them in clean coverings, before carrying them to the boat.

When canning the salmon strips, we formed an assembly line starting with wiping the oil and smoke off the fish. The next person had to cut the tips off then pass it to the next who cut the strips to the size of the can. The tips and ends were saved for eating also. Filling the cans was next, then the lids were put on and last was sealing the lids with a sealer. The strips were weighed before putting them in cans to make sure each can had the right weight for selling. Having a big family was rewarding, since there were many of us to help with this project. It wasn't all fun and cooperation though, as sometimes arguments would break out among us.

After all the preparations were done, moving day, back to Holy Cross from fishcamp, was suddenly here. When we were ready to move, we had to wait for a sunny, calm day. Sometimes we had to wait a couple of days if it was windy or rainy. At times it took us about a week to get ready for the move. We were all anxious to get back to civilization, so we were all willing to work long hours each day.

The excitement of living in camp all summer is worn out and we are all ready for the village. We even washed our hair (sometimes) and set our curlers on (tin strips cut out from milk cans, wrapped with catalog paper) to make ourselves beautiful. Everyone would go to bed and the excitement of moving kept us awake talking and planning for our trip. The anticipation of moving and weather checking, took up our evening.

Then finally morning came and everything had to be carried down the bank and loaded into the boat. We sometimes had a barge like boat that was used to "haul" the fish in. Our boat was attached to the back of the barge to push it. Sometimes, we had the fish loaded the day before the actual move so on moving day we only had our personal items to take care of. But carrying the bundles of fish, cases of bottled fish, berries and jams, rolling barrels of berries, salt fish, and other things took us several hours to do.

Lastly, the dogs had to be put in the boat and tied for their safety. Their excited barks and impatient yelps as we tried to restrain them, filled the quiet fishcamp surroundings.

Leaving camp at summers end was sometimes sad. Everything looked lonesome and quiet after all the summer noises of living there with the daily busy living activities.

Then off we were to the village. I guess the load we had made us travel slow because it seemed we took hours to reach the village. When we were loading the boat, we each claimed a favorite spot to sit in the boat while traveling. We piled boxes and bedding to make comfortable cushioned seats where we sat covered with a coat to keep warm.

Sometimes we would get caught in a rain storm, so dad would put a tarp up to form cover over the boat for us to stay under. This was kind of boring because not being able to see where we were going made the trip seem longer. Dad would be steering the boat so he had to be out in the rain. He would be standing by the steering wheel wearing his rain gear. Standing helped keep him dryer as the rain would run off the rain gear. But I'm sure it was tiring, damp and cold.

Half way between camp and the village we stopped to make "tea" and have lunch. If it was raining we all sat in the boat under the make shift tent and ate. Crackers or biscuits and fish strips washed down with cold tea was our lunch. If the weather was nice we would stop on the sand bar and make a campfire. Dad cut willows and made a device to hang the water kettle over the fire and we all shared hot tea with our food. This was better than the cold tea on rainy days.

Several hours after leaving camp we finally reached the village. In the earlier years when we lived at the end of the village, we had to carry all our belongings to our house. We lived in the old log cabin at the end of the village about a five minute walk back from the river bank where our boat was. Wheelbarrows and an old two wheel cart were loaded with supplies and we would pair up to haul the "stuff".

In the spring, before moving to fishcamp, a cache was prepared to store our winter food in. At the end of summer all our fish and berries were put there. The cache was filled and ready for the long, cold winter.

When we moved to our new house above the village, dad would borrow the mission truck to haul our goods. This made life a little simpler. We loaded everything we could on the truck and rode on the back of it to the house. Then we unloaded everything and carried them to the house or cache.

At the end of all that we were pretty worn out, but we still managed to run to the movie or visit friends in the evening. If we happened to move to the village on a Sunday, then we were able to attend the weekly Sunday movie. Before we left the house we all had to wash ourselves and change clothes. After the careful preparations we took to groom ourselves the night before moving, then doing the moving work all day, we probably looked and smelled pretty bad.

Even though the end of summer was here, we still had a lot of winter preparations to do.

In August my parents would set nets for the silvers that would "run" about the middle of that month. In the village we would have a small smoke house to cut and smoke the fish. Mom also pressure cooked cases of the silvers in mason jars for winter use.

During the Fall moose hunting season, all the village men traveled to surrounding areas by boat for their annual hunting. Dad was gone for several days, and returning, he would have a nice fat moose.

One year, when one of my brothers was born, in mid September, dad had taken a nap. When he woke up, he shared a dream he had about getting a moose. He quickly got ready to go hunting, and taking the boat traveled below the village to a small slough. There he spotted a moose and shot it. He returned to the village for us to help him cut and carry the meat to the boat. I remember having a small bucket which dad would fill with small parts of meat for me to carry to the boat. It took us a while, but we got the whole moose loaded in the boat and taken back to the village. The slough was promptly named " birthday slough" because of the brother who was born that day.

The moose would be cut into small pieces and put into jars for pressure cooking. We didn't have freezers, so this was one way of keeping the meat from spoiling. The cases of jarred moose meat was kept in the cellar under our cabin, along with the other cases of jarred geese, fish, vegetables, sacks of potatoes and berry jams.

In our cabin, in the middle of the room floor there was a small trap door. Opening this we could jump down into a small cellar that was used to store the cases of food. Sometimes, in the cellar, we could see or hear the many mice that made this area under the cabin their permanent home.

Moose fat was used to make lard. The fat was cooked in a pot for several hours, then the fat would be separated and saved in jars for cooking use. I never was able to get used to moose fat lard, which had a wild taste to it. It made pancakes taste bad.

Hunting for geese and ducks took place in the Fall also. Again, for storage, the geese and ducks were cooked in pressure cooked jars and kept in our cellar.

One winter preparation I enjoyed doing was cutting dry grass for dog houses. Usually a Saturday morning or afternoon, or time after school on weekdays, was spent in the field below the village. Using a knife we cut the tall grass at the bottom and tied them together with strands of grass to make a large bundle. Grass cutting was done until there were enough bundles to last the winter. The supply was stored under the cache to keep dry. During winter months dog houses were kept warm and dry with weekly changes of the grass.

The dry grass was also used for insoles in our mukluks or boots.

Wood cutting also had to be done in the Fall. Traveling out of the village by boat was the usual way to get the needed wood. Dry logs were cut about 4 to 5 feet long. The wood was measured in a pile called a "cord". Sometimes wood would be sold between families. Everyone had large piles of wood outside their houses.

The usual scenario near each house was a saw horse for sawing the logs into blocks. Then there was the wood cutting block used to chop the wood into sizes to fit into the stove. The chopped wood was carried and piled in the house by the stove against the wall. Sometimes we had so much wood it would reach almost to the ceiling. In our old house we had a big porch in the front to pile chopped wood in also.

Then it was time for black/blueberry picking. Blueberries were usually ready in mid to late August. Sometimes we traveled and camped out for several days, or even a week to do the berry picking. These were fun times if the weather was good. Traveling in sloughs, listening to loons at night or watching animals, as we sat on hillsides picking berries, were experiences that could not be replaced or forgotten. Flocks of geese and ducks could be seen and heard far off, or sometimes flying over us, as they sent their gathering calls to each other. Other strange wild call noises

Grandma Erena holding my daughter Michelle.
Taken in 1972 in Holy Cross.

could be heard at night and sometimes we would wonder what they were. Maybe loons or other wild animals. Frogs were heard all day and all night, especially in fishcamp, and in the village also.

Black/red berries (called winter berries) were picked in early September. By that time the weather would be starting to turn colder, especially at night.

One of my favorite berry picking trips was taken by my cousin and I with an older couple, Erena and Victor Woods. The old lady was related to dad, but they were like grandparents to us.

It was early September when we left the village. Their boat was large with a house over it. Dad had them tow our boat alongside for us to sleep in. Canvas tarping was used to cover the top to keep the cold and rain out.

We traveled across from the village on the Yukon River to the slough that led to the Innoko river. Then we traveled up the Innoko River for several hours to reach a favorite picking area. The berry area was called Bishops mountain. We stopped by several sloughs before finally settling in one that we thought might have berries. It was late when we landed so we prepared for evening by fixing supper and getting ready for bed.

Supper was ducks that were shot earlier. We were told by grandma Erena, to pluck the ducks and clean them in preparation for cooking. Taking things into our own hands we plucked the feathers, opened the stomachs and cleaned the intestines out and threw everything over the boat side into the slough. We then gave her the prepared birds. She was surprised we had got the ducks ready for cooking and telling us we did well, asked what we did with the "bowels". Threw them into the slough we said. This made her laugh, but we didn't know why she thought that was funny. We laughed when she referred to the duck intestines as "bowels". We never heard anyone using that expression on duck intestines before. Or maybe it was the way she said it. Anyway the soup she prepared was delicious, especially eating it, sitting in the open part of the boat, as dusk was falling, with everything quiet except for the wild noises. So peaceful and calm was the surrounding land.

The first night my cousin and I slept in our boat. The old couple and their grandson slept in their own boat next to ours. The night was long and cold. I welcomed the morning when we got up and went into their boat which was equipped with a small wood stove. It was warm and we welcomed the cup of tea they gave us along with a nice hot breakfast.

The next night they decided it was too cold for us to sleep in our boat, so they invited us to spend the night in their boat. Their boat was pretty crowded with supplies, clothes and bedding piled everywhere. My bed was the narrow wooden seat (across the width of the boat). It was made wider by piling boxes side by side next to the seat. I fixed my blankets to make a fairly comfortable bed and slept soundly all night. It was much warmer and I felt safer.

The next morning I woke to hear talking and morning preparations. They had a nice fire going in the small stove, so it was warm and toasty under the blankets. Laying there with my eyes closed, I listened to the old folks talking and moving around. It sounded like they were looking for something. Finally I asked them what they were looking for. The bacon for breakfast could not be found. I laid in my bed listening to them talking and searching for a time. Then I decided to help them. Getting out of bed I rolled up by pillow and blankets. Guess what was under my pillow. The lost bacon. This was very funny to them and I was teased for some time about using bacon for my pillow.

After breakfast we packed lunch which consisted of tea, fish strips and sometimes canned vegetables, and walked up the hill looking for berries. We made a back pack out of gunny sacks and put a gas can in it for berries we would pick. The cans were square about one foot in diameter and about a foot and a half high. We also had smaller buckets to pick with and when full dumped the berries into the larger container. Sometimes the ground looked red or black when there were a lot of berries. The black berries were mixed in along with the red berries. We spend the whole day picking and eating berries. Returning to the boat the old couple would laugh and wonder out loud why our mouths were so black. They teased us about eating more berries than we picked.

Lunch time was fun up in the mountain. We never built a fire up there, so we usually had a cold lunch. It seemed to me the food tasted delicious as we sat on the soft moss in the cool sunny weather. We would take about a half hour sitting around eating and talking.

This was where I tried my very first cigarette, but I'm glad I never picked up that bad habit. After eating lunch, grandma Erena offered us a cigarette which we happily accepted. I usually wasn't one to do something this daring. We happily lit up the cigarette and smoked it. She told us not to put it out in the ground, but to let her know when we were done and she would show us a trick to put cigarettes out. When we were done we let her know and walking over to us, she spit into her hands, taking our cigarettes she doused them out in it. We laughed about that little trick, thinking it was pretty funny, but clever.

By the end of the day we had our storage cans pretty well filled with berries. We probably would have more if we didn't take so many breaks, running around and tumbling in the moss. We also ate a lot of the berries we should have been picking.

As we returned to the boat we took turns carrying our back pack, filled with berries, down the mountain. It was fun walking down hill, much easier then climbing up. While one of us carried the berries the other would tumble on down the hill on the soft moss. This was so much fun. Finally reaching the boat we were exhausted from the walking and tumbling. We stored the picked berries in an empty wooden gas can box.

After the evening meal, we sat around in the boat talking and listening to stories told by the old people. Their stories were fun and interesting to listen to. Some sounded a little far fetched but I always believed what I was told about their early days. They were wise people and gave us good advice.

After about a week of berry picking, it was time to return to the village. Even though it was fun and we enjoyed being out, we always looked forward anxiously to returning home.

Chapter 9

Other berry picking trips were taken with our whole family. Food, gas, bedding and tents were packed in preparation for the trip and then the hope for good traveling weather.

We traveled the same route as with the old couple, but to a different location. When we reached this camping site, tents were put up and our camp was readied for staying a few days.

We camped at the mouth of a small slough leading to a lake. The lake was surrounded by small mountains, which we climbed to pick berries. Daily for about three days we picked, berries unrelentingly.

In the evenings we rested, or played games on the small sandbar next to our camp. Sometimes dad made fishhooks, out of a bent nail, tied with string to a willow pole. We set this fishhook over the side of the boat and sat, waiting patiently for our catch. We actually would catch the small pike that swam from the main river to the lake. Mom would cook this up and make Indian ice cream with the fresh berries we picked. The Indian ice cream was always a delicious treat for us. The men went hunting for the geese that were flying in the lake area. Then we had fresh geese soup for our dinner.

The Indian ice cream was a mixture of melted lard (shortening), unmelted lard, fish broth or water, sugar and berries. The fish was cooked then deboned and flaked. This mixture was rinsed with a small amount of water, then the water had to be squeezed out hand full at a time. The fish was mixed with the oil and water/broth until soft and fluffy. Sugar was added for taste and lastly berries and sometimes raisins was added.

Daily we walked up the surrounding hills to spend the day picking berries. I chose a site where there were bunches of berries and sat there for hours filling up my container. One year I was concentrating so much on picking berries that I didn't watch where I was going. Suddenly I was surrounded by "Yellow Jackets", those hated hornets. They were buzzing all around and on me. One was on my thumb, holding on to me and the sting was so bad I screamed and shook him off. I ran away to the area my parents were and told them what had happened. My thumb, by that time was real sore and swollen. No one worried about it, so I forgot about it and continued picking berries. It's a good thing I didn't have bee allergies, as no one knew anything about allergies at that time, so we didn't have things like bee sting kits handy.

When it was lunch time we all sat around on the mossy ground sharing our food and listening to stories our parents told. A favorite topic was about mountain people. Many stories were told of mountain people, but I was not sure if I believed these stories or not. My parents told us stories that came from their parents who believed mountain people lived there.

One saying was that we should not leave our belongings laying around because when we looked for them, we would not find them. It was because the mountain people had taken them.

Another story about mountain people was told by grandma Savage to mom. Several family members, including grandma, grandpa, dad, other relatives and friends were going berry picking a little above our fishcamp in a small slough. Climbing up the mountain they came to a small clear spot on the ground. Looking closely, they saw many small huts with one large one in the middle of the others. They left a few sticks of matches there and continued on their berry picking climb. When they were returning down the hill, they stopped by the clear spot to check out the small huts. Smoke was coming out of the larger hut, probably the Kashim.

I always liked this story, but never quite sure if I believed it or not.

The usual blue or blackberry area we went to was located on the Innoko River. This river lead to the village of Shageluk, where mom was born and raised in.

One year, during a berry picking trip, we went to Shageluk and spent several days there. It was fun to visit with our aunt, uncle and cousins. This was the year I saved my whole 50 cents given to me on my birthday in December. I planned to spend it on candy in the village store. While we were camping out I lost it in the willows but my family helped me search for the small tin can I kept it in. We walked through the willow patch until we finally found my treasured 50 cents. To me that was a lot of money in those days.

In the village of Shageluk, we traveled by canoes across the lake behind the village to the blueberry area. One day it was raining so hard, but that didn't deter us hardy berry pickers. We walked in the wet rainy area and picked all day. The berries were large, blue and delicious. One of my favorite things to do after blueberry picking was to fix a bowl of mashed berries mixed with sugar and milk. That mixture made a delicious sort of blueberry milk shake.

A short diversionary story of visiting in Shageluk. The year this happened, we stayed with my auntie. One day she set up her outdoor stove and started cooking a large pot of moose soup. As it was cooking, my younger cousin threw in several pieces of old clams he had found in the small lake behind the village. This made auntie pretty angry as she picked the old clam shells out of her cooking pot. It's a good thing it didn't ruin our moose dinner. I wondered if those clams could have been poisonous, but I guess not, since we all survived eating the soup.

When returning to Holy Cross, the berries were prepared for winter by storing them in sealed barrels and kept in the cache. The winter berries (red and black) were stored in wooden boxes and covered securely with canvas or plastic. The cold winter weather kept the berries frozen.

Other berry picking activities were done in the village. Below the village in the woods, there were patches of rosehips, cranberries, red and black currents and raspberries. Villagers made it a habit to pick these berries each fall for making jam. When we lived in our old log cabin at the end of the village, we walked a little down the road or in the woods across from our cabin to pick berries. The wooded area across our cabin was filled with red current bushes that were filled with the clear red berries. Rose hips were everywhere in the woods below the village. These berries made delicious jam.

One day, when we were in our early teens, my sister and I decided we were going berry picking. Mom was in the hospital at Bethel and dad was looking after us. Walking down the road into the woods to look for berries, we came upon a pig pen the mission kept there. The pig pen was large, with a small wooden house in the middle and surrounded with tree poles as a fence. We decided to tease the pigs, so we made them run round and round in the pen after us. When they were running fast, we jumped out of the pen and grabbed a tree branch and held onto it until the pigs were close. Then we let go the branches slapping them in the face. We thought it was so funny as we listened to their angry squeals and we laughed and laughed, repeating the process over and over. The pigs didn't seem to learn their lesson and would chase us each time. We also ran round and round in the pig pen and when the pigs were fast after us we ran into their house and slammed the door. Their small wooden house was in the center of the pen. Finally, when they gave up looking for us we would open the door and run to the fence, jumping over to safety. This was a dangerous game, which we didn't know at that time, but it was fun teasing the animals.

When I was older (in my mid teens), I sometimes accompanied grandma Erena, in late Fall walking below the village around the hill. There were many small hills and streams back there and pretty anytime of the year. In the Fall trees were leafless and the ones that had leaves were colorful with their red, yellow and brown Fall colors. We walked and walked until we reached the spots to pick berries. Black or red fall berries were sometimes found, but not a lot. We picked berries all day and would get a half of a bucket full. But just the walk and the outing, having lunch as we sat on the soft moss, was enough to satisfy our craving for being in the outside one last time before the winter coldness and snow set in.

These are special times to remember, walking, listening to late geese calling to each other, watching for woods animals. We never carried a gun for protection, but Grandma Erena would tell me to watch out for bears. If we saw one, I was to stay still, not panic and everything would be fine. Sometimes, we would take a piece of wood and hit it against our picking pots, to scare away animals she told me.

She shared a story with me about her childhood days when she was berry picking with elders. One day some of the women were out in the hills alone. A bear came upon them and they had no gun for protection. They all sat down on the ground, staying still and not moving. The bear walked around and around and up to them, throwing dirt and snorting on them. They still didn't move, so finally the bear walked off, but he continued to watch them by looking back under his arms so they wouldn't see him looking. They sat still until he was out of site, then quickly gathered their things and rushed back to the village.

Another berry picking adventure to remember was when the missionaries lived in the village. Every fall the missionaries would select a few of the mission kids and load them into a large barge for the berry picking trip. One year, dad said my sister and I could go with the missionaries on one of their berry picking trips.

On the day of travel we had to get up real early, five or six in the morning. We walked to the mission to attend mass before the trip.

Then we all walked to the bluff above the mission where the boat was. There was their big house boat with a large barge in front. The kids and missionaries all piled into the barge and claimed comfortable sitting places. Everyone was excited about the traveling adventure which would take all day. Leaving the village we traveled across the Yukon to a slough that led to the Inokko River. We traveled to the favorite berry picking place called "Bishop's Mountain". Here we climbed the hills to spend our day berry picking.

The missionaries provided everyone with a lunch of sandwiches, dried fish, kool aid or tea. In the evening we traveled back to the village. It was a long trip, and for entertainment, the nuns had us tell stories, and sing songs. That was a fun and unforgettable trip.

Another Fall activity which took place by villagers was blackfish trapping in the many small sloughs below the village. Men would make blackfish traps out of narrow strips of wood. The trap was narrow at one end and wide mouthed with narrow strips of wood blocking the entrance at the front. Once the fish swam in they had no way to exit. These traps were set in the sloughs or creeks below the village. The fish were small and bony but tasty. Some were stored for winter use and also for dog food.

Fall hunting for willow grouse "black chicken" was fun. When we were younger, mom and dad would let us go with them to hunt for the willow grouse. They would walk up the hill behind the village and far into the wooded area searching for the birds. Sometimes we would startle the willow grouse and they would suddenly fly near us scaring or surprising us with their wing noises and screams of surprise.

Our parents didn't allow us to use guns or to go into the woods to hunt alone. But when I was in my late teens, a friend and I would sometimes sneak out to hunt on Sundays when everyone was in the weekly movie, or after school when I was supposed to be visiting her. She would take her .22 gun and we walked around the hill to the woods to hunt.

Willow grouse would fly from tree to tree finally landing, that was when we would shoot and sometimes be lucky enough to get one. These birds lived off of eating pine needles, and when we plucked the feathers, the sack under their neck would be full of the needles. The meat tasted piney, but was good when roasted with onions, that is if we were lucky enough to have onions.

During the winter ptarmigan was seen flying across the sandbar area where people went to hunt for them also.

Another delicious food was rabbit which villagers hunted for or trapped during winter months. Traveling with dog sled dad would go out for a day and return with about a dozen or so rabbits. We had to skin them and that was a job I didn't like.

Sometimes we set rabbit snares across the road from our house or in the back wooded area. That was when we lived in our old house at the end of the village. Being at the end of the village the woods was handy with lots of trees all around us and across the small road. Early in the morning before going to school and returning in the afternoon we would run into the woods to check our snares. Sometimes we would be lucky and get a rabbit or two. Mom and dad would be proud of our efforts and would tell other people who we invited to eat with us, that we were the lucky trappers who provided the meal.

A little of the Nuns and girls house. The church is next with the village in the back. The gardens are on front. The river used to come to the bank but now the front where the river was is all a large willow tree forest. On the left side is a part of the old hospital building.

Chapter 10

Before the mission closed down, moving away from the village, they had large gardens planted around the hillside and mission area. The potato/vegetable gardens were located in front of the sisters house, the church and in the area below the church and the whole hillside. Houses are now located throughout the old garden areas.

Some parts of the garden area was previously used for dog pens. The mission had many dogs, which were tied next to their small dog houses on both side of the road below the mission buildings and before reaching the village. There were dog pens and dogs everywhere. They were pretty noisy and smelly at times.

Planting time was fun to watch. The missionaries, with the help of mission kids would plow and hoe all day, dropping potato cutlets in the ground and covering them. Before planting time, kids and missionaries would cut potatoes into small pieces for planting.

After the missionaries moved away, during school days, we were sometimes allowed to help with cutting potatoes readying them for planting. We cut the potatoes to small sizes, instructed to leave eyes in each piece for growing. After the initial mission closure, a few of the nuns and brothers, and priests were left behind to take care of the buildings and attend to daily church activities for the villagers.

When the potatoes were growing, the fields were filled with green potato leaves and usually surrounded with weeds. During the summer we would see missionaries and kids kneeling on the ground weeding and cleaning the gardens daily.

Harvesting potatoes and vegetables took place in September. The missionaries used a tractor to plow for the potatoes with kids following behind carrying gunny sacks to pick the overturned potatoes. Sacks and sacks would be picked and stored in the cellar of the sisters house. There were large bins there filled with potatoes, cabbage, turnips and carrots.

When the mission was done with their plowing and picking of potatoes, villagers were allowed to dig in the gardens for left over potatoes. With gunny sacks and shovels we would pick a spot and dig for the potatoes. On a sunny Fall day, you could see villagers working throughout the garden areas with their shovels and gunny sacks. We sometimes returned home with two or three gunny sacks full of potatoes.

Villagers also had their own small gardens, usually located near or in the back of their house area. When we lived at the end of the village in our old house our potato garden was located on top of the bank. We had a path which led through the woods to our garden, and to my cousins house located across from the garden.

Near our house, we had another smaller garden used for smaller vegetables such as carrots, cabbages, lettuce and turnips. Leaf lettuce was grown instead of the head lettuce.

We ate the lettuce dipped in sugar, since we didn't have salad dressing at that time. It tasted good with the sugar.

Digging and turning over the ground had to be done manually with a shovel. This was an all day task which took several days. During the later part of May, villagers could be seen digging and turning over the dirt in their individual gardens throughout the village. After turning over the ground, we had to let the soil dry. Next came the part of hoeing or chopping up the ground readying it for planting. We made rows for planting with walks in between.

Then potatoes had to be planted. We helped our parents with all these tasks. When I was younger, about ten or eleven, I was chosen to stay at the house with younger children, and to fix supper for everyone. The first meal I fixed was mashed potatoes and jarred moose meat or fish. The potatoes were a success and tasted pretty good, as I received congratulations from my parents on the delicious meal I had fixed them.

When I was older I was promoted from house help to gardening activities.

The new house Dad built in the mid 1950's.

In our new house above the mission, we had a garden along the hillside below our house. The garden was large and took a long time to dig up, plant and then weed during summer.

When we were at fishcamp, a few days in July had to be set aside for traveling to the village for weeding and tending the garden.

Weeding was always a hated job by all of us. We spend about two days doing this menial task. Mosquitoes and gnats had fun chewing at and pestering us. Sometimes we built small fires in an old pot or tin can and covered the fire with grass or weeds. This made heavy smoke which the pestering insects didn't like. It helped us, except for our burning eyes from the smoke.

After the fall winter preparation was done, all we had to do was wait for cold snowy days. What fun those days were. The clean snow covered everything and made trees beautiful and white. The frozen mud on the roads from rainy fall days was covered with the snow. This made walking hard, until the snow was packed down from our daily walks to school and from dog sleds traveling. Everything would be quiet and still and seemed to be holding its breath from the cold.

In November, about Thanksgiving time, eels were caught. Men and boys traveled on the river below the village. They made holes in the river ice to dip for the eels. The weather about that time was usually very cold, but people still did their jobs of food getting. Dad would come home with a sled full of these skinny, slimy, black snake like looking things.

But they were real tasty, especially when baked, covered in onions, in the oven, kind of like sardines.

Eels were also used for dog food which gave them a change in diet from the everyday use of fish.

Older village people had a belief that if there was a death in a family, the family was not allowed to hunt for eels. Eels had the feeling of death and would disappear the minute the family member started dipping. Mom, dad and other village elders said this happened on several occasions.

White fish and lush were dipped for during winter months. Men and boys traveled on the river and made large holes on the ice. Using large dip nets, people would get many fish if the run was good. Again, dad would come home with a sled full of fish. I wasn't really crazy for eating the white fish, but they did make good Indian ice cream. Lush was delicious with cooked beans and was a favorite to me.

During winter months, dad kept one of the white fish frozen on top of the porch for eating. Every once in a while, he would bring it in the house to slice pieces for a snack. He shared some with us kids, but mom didn't like us eating raw fish. She was afraid it would make us sick.

Fur trapping was done in November for about a month. Dad would travel to his trapline about that time, returning just before Christmas. Traveling with the dog team, he left the village and traveled all day until he reached his trapline. Usually there would be a trapping buddy, a friend to share the line, fur and work.

For days, before dad left for trapping, preparations were made. Warm clothes were packed, food prepared, harnesses mended, sleds, skis and snowshoes were mended and dog food packed. Mom baked baking powder biscuits, prepared burger out of ground moose meat and fixed cooked beans. All these were packed in flour sacks and kept frozen.

Dad would bring the sled in the house to thaw out and be checked for mending. Dripping melted ice and snow would fall on the floor until the sled was finally dry. Then he would work on it until it was fit for travel again.

Finally the day of departure came. Sometimes, dad would ride in front of the sled on a pair of skies, holding on to a long pole attached to the sled. This was called a "G" pole. He was an expert at riding this way and never seemed to be nervous, or fall. He also rode the "G" pole when he traveled to the wood cutting camp.

A short story of dad riding the "G" pole was told by mom. In her and dad's first married days, there were winter activities such as dog races and ski races held. Villagers would watch from the hillside as the men raced over the banks toward the village from the sandbar area. Dad would be racing on a pair of skis' pulled by the dogs. Grandma told mom "don't watch him" meaning dad, as it would be bad luck and he would fall or not win. Once mom took a peek and sure enough just as she did, dad took a fall and that ended his race for that time.

Reaching his trapline, dad pitched a tent and stored all his "goodies" for safety. Dogs were tied around the camp and grass or branches were placed under them for warmth. In the tent, branches or dried grass were also placed under the bedding for warmth and dryness. A small yukon stove was used in the tent for warmth and cooking.

Our dog team was pretty special in those days. I remember one lead dog we had whose name was "Sparky". He had one blue eye. Sparky was a smart, dependable and gentle dog, understanding dads every command. He was also a special friend to us all. When traveling home to the village after trapping or hunting, dad would say "go home Sparky". Understanding "home" the dog would pick up speed and head happily toward the village.

One year while geese hunting, dad sprained his back on the way home. In the Spring the snow was partially melted and going up a bank in part mud and snow, he helped the dogs by pushing the sled. This caused the sprain. He was in a lot of pain and couldn't stand behind the sled, so he climbed into the sled and told "Sparky" to take him home. They did make it home safely and we were all grateful to the dog who we all felt was our best friend.

Years later when Sparky was growing old, one day in fishcamp he disappeared. Dad told us Sparky had run away and he pretended to look for him up and down the river. In later years I realized Sparky was put away because of his health and age.

Dad had a sled full of geese that he had to lay on. When reaching the village he had to be carried into the house. He was bedridden in back pain for several weeks.

Meanwhile, the geese he got had to be taken care of. This was a yearly Spring and Fall activity. We spent several days plucking feathers and cleaning "guts". Plucking geese was one of my least favorite things to do. My fingers, especially thumb, would be real sore after doing several of the fowl. I hated when the small lice from the birds would be running up my hand or arm. They were real fast but we had to be faster to catch them.

After we were finished plucking the geese, they were cut into pieces, expertly by mom. She filled mason jars with the parts, and cooked them in a pressure cooker. The pressured cooked geese were kept for future use in the same way we did the summer jarred fish and moose.

The jarred geese and moose made a delicious soup. Potatoes and vegetables would be cooked and when done, the jarred item was added. The juice in the jar made a good flavored broth. Jarred moose had the same results.

When I was in my teens, my parents would be out wood cutting, berry picking, or doing gardening. They sometimes left me in charge of the smaller kids and fixing supper. When they were due to return, I cooked the potatoes and vegetables in a pot and added the jarred moose or geese. Upon returning, my parents would congratulate me on the delicious meal I had ready for them.

All the work we did was done for survival. Subsistence fishing and hunting was important to everyday living in the village and people depended on that lifestyle. Even during fishing season everyone used what they needed without waste. We didn't fish, only for the biggest fish for trophies or for throwing small ones back or leaving to waste on shore. People took good care of their meat catches too. When trapping, furs were kept neatly packed and not allowed to be left laying around uncared for. There was a strictness and respect for food because of the elders telling us about past starvations.

People always shared their catches with others in the village, especially with elders.

One of the nice habits of villagers is that people never let visitors go away hungry. Everyone who visited our house, being from the village or out of town, were given meals or sometimes a cup of tea with bread or crackers. Salmon strips, and other dried fish were shared with them.

My parents always shared, what food we had, with older folks in the village. They invited the older folks or single older men to share meals. When dad got a moose, he would give some to the older folks. He also would share moose, fish and fowl with the mission when they were at the village, before moving away.

Sometimes my parents would send me to the older people to "call" them for supper. Calling them was an invitation. Since we didn't have phones, walking to their house was the way of giving our invitation.

There was this old blind man my parents would "call" for supper every once in a while. I had to go to his house to do the invitation. When it was time for dinner, I had to get him and lead him to our house by holding the end of his cane. After eating, I delivered him safely home. Sometimes I would catch myself walking fast, forgetting that maybe he needed to walk a little slower. He was always a kind, gracious and appreciative old man.

Another old couple lived down the road from our house. They were pretty old, and in my early years, (maybe about six or seven years old) I was afraid of them. So afraid, that if I met them on the road, I would detour off the road into the grass and wait for them to pass by. Hopefully I didn't hurt their feelings, but they didn't seem to pay attention to me hiding in the grass.

After getting a little older I was rid of my fear of them, and would go to their house to invite them for meals or bring them a special dish mom fixed of geese, rabbit, moose soup or Native ice cream. The little old grandma would show her appreciation for the little food gifts, by giving me a sugar cube. She talked only the Indian language, and talking to me she would hold my face between her hands and say whatever she felt she had to say to thank me. Not understanding the Indian language, I smiled at her and nodded my head in agreement to everything she said. She was a tiny cute little old lady with two blue lines (tattoos) on her chin. I noticed a lot of the older ladies at that time had blue lines on their chin that was done when they were small children. Some of them even had earring holes on their ears. Most of them wore thin nets around their hair.

There were other older people and bachelors my parents invited for meals. I enjoyed having these people over, listening to them talk and tell stories.

Sometimes dad would share homebrew with some of the local men or bachelors. One old bachelor used to spend hours visiting and having the brew. After having his fill he would get a little loud and argumentative. When we girls thought he was getting a little carried away, we would run him out of the house. We sometimes physically handled him right out of the door, with coat and hat following. Sometimes we ran him up the road, or when we moved to our new house, down the road. After those incidents, we returned to the house, laughing at our deed, thinking how funny it was to see him so afraid of us small skinny girls.

I have to share with you the incident that happened in our fishcamp one year. It was the fourth of July and we had visited the upper fishcamp. Dad started having homebrew with these two men. When he had enough, we left for our fishcamp. A little later, a boat came by with his two drinking companions. They wanted to land their boat, but we girls didn't want them to bring anymore "drink" to our dad. We stationed ourselves on each side of the small landing slough, under the bank, in front of our camp. With long poles we pushed their boat out each time they tried to land on shore. Wet mud balls were thrown, hitting them and landing in their boat. We had a lot of fun trying to scare them away.

Finally, after about fifteen minutes of this rough treatment to the men, dad found out what we were doing. I guess he heard their yells for help. Stopping us, he let the men land their boat and come to shore. The two were pretty well into their cups and started an argument and fight with dad. But we girls wouldn't let a good fight pass us by so we jumped right in and ganged up on the two men, hitting, kicking, biting, scratching and finally running them down to their boat with large fish hanging poles. One of them got hit in the back with a pole. He had had enough of this torture and yelled to the other to get to the boat. The other was a little tougher and wanted to pick a fight with us. But his companion would have none of that and took him running down the bank to the boat and shoving off for safety.

When they left shore, the tougher fellow wanted to return to our camp. They started an argument in the middle of the river and started fighting in their boat, drifting downriver.

For several hours, my parents worried about where they were, as they didn't return upriver. Finally dad sent my uncle to look for them. Several hours later he returned, laughingly telling us they were in the camp below our camp. They were visiting and drinking coffee with folks in that camp. I was glad they had a happy ending to their Fourth of July. The two men didn't return to our camp. I guess they had had enough of us tough "Savage" girls.

I guess we girls were protectors to dad against any of the men in the village. If they got into their "cup" of brew and wanted to pick fights, we would step right in and help dad to scare them off. None of them wanted to mess with us girls.

Chapter 11

At the beginning of the book I talked about living in the fishcamp year round with grandparents and relatives. The reason they moved to the village was because we girls were old enough to start school.

My grandparents, aunt and uncle moved along with us to the village. We all settled in a nice spot located down the road, at the end of the village. My grandparents' small log cabin was the last house in the village, facing our cabin across a small yard. A little above, up the road was Auntie Martha's cabin.

The small cabin we lived in had two rooms, separating living room/kitchen from the bedroom with a partition. We lived there until my grandparents both passed away in about 1948 and 1949.

We then moved in my grandparents cabin for several years. Since it was too small for our yearly growing family, dad decided to add an extension to the back of the cabin. So for several Fall days, we traveled by boat to an area below the village on the banks of the Yukon river. Here we spent days cutting pine tree logs for the house. Mom would pack a lunch of dried fish, cans of beans, carrots or other vegetables, crackers and tea, for us to share while spending the day with dad.

The logs were striped of bark and branches. They were put into the river and tied together in a raft and towed to the village by boat.

Dad set to adding the new addition to our log cabin. Windows were put in place. There were two windows, one on the road side and one on the back. Inside walls were covered with cardboard, as we were poor and didn't have material for siding.

I remember hearing mice running between the wall and the paper siding. Sometimes laying in bed at night, we could hear the busy activities of the mice. They were so bold that one even bit dad on the nose one night while he was asleep in bed. After that many traps were set throughout the cabin and cellar.

A heater stove, half of a tin barrel, was used for heating the additional cabin.

Moss was used for insulating the cracks between the logs. By boat, we traveled above the village along the river to a mountain side. We climbed to the mossy areas and filled gunny sacks full with moss. When we had enough bags of moss, we returned to the village. Dad then used the moss to cover the cracks between logs of the cabin. This done, dad made some sort of mixture out of mud and cement to put over the moss. The base of the outside of the house, ground area, was banked with mud for warmth. The roof was of boards covered with sheet iron.

The sheet iron roof was perfect for catching rain water which we used for laundry or scrubbing floors and dishes.

The house was the perfect size for us to play "Red Rover", which we did many times.

The first days I could remember probably in the late 1940's, we had no electricity in the village. We had to light our homes with a lantern which was pretty dim and we had light only in the main room. Later in the early fifty's we graduated to the gas lamp, which gave a brighter light. The gas lamp had two "mantles" like light bulbs. These mantles were very delicate and had to be treated carefully. If we touched or jerked them they would crumble into ashes.

A few years later, in the mid 1950's we finally had electricity, but only for a limited time during the day. Usually the lights would come on about 7:00 a.m. and be turned off 11:30 p.m. During the day the electricity would be turned off during certain hours to save fuel.

If we had washing machines, run by electricity, we had to do laundry quickly when the electricity was turned on. Before we had electricity and washing machines, laundry was done with the washtub and washboards. Clothes were scrubbed individually on the washboard. They were then put into another tub to be rinsed and hand-wringed before hanging out in the clothesline. Later in years, we somehow got a wringer that had to be hand turned, but it was a big improvement over hand wringing clothes and getting blisters. As I mentioned before, this was especially hard to do in fishcamp. When we were younger, with small brothers, we had to have wash day for two or three days a week ending up with many blisters on our small hands.

We didn't have to worry about ironing with electric irons, because the irons we used were the heavy cast iron type, heated on top of the stove. We had about two or three of these so we could trade off and use one while the others were heating. Every Saturday, I enjoyed ironing my brothers shirts for them to wear to Sunday mass.

Other Saturday chores I enjoyed doing when I was in my teens, was to bake a large pan of bread. I had six younger brothers, so by Sunday afternoon the bread would be all gone. The rest of the week we had baking power biscuits or crackers. In between baking bread, I also scrub floors, do the weekly laundry mixed in with ironing. So by evening, sometimes, I would be too tired to eat my supper. But I still had to attend the Saturday evening benediction at church and go to weekly confession after. I don't know why I had to go to confession. God should have forgiven me what sins I might have committed after doing the heavy chores all day without complaining even.

Holy Cross was founded in 1857 by a Catholic priest. The story I heard was that the priest stopped in Anvik, a small village about 30 miles above Holy Cross on the banks of the Yukon River. The Episcopal missionaries had already started a mission there, but they told him they knew a spot below their village that was nice for a settlement.

So traveling there, about 30 - 35 miles below Anvik, with a guide the present village of Holy Cross was founded.

Holy Cross is located on the banks of the Yukon River, surrounded half way in the back by hills. The mission was located at the upper part of the village closer to the hill. On top of the hill was a big white wooden cross to depict the name of the village.

When the village was started by missionaries, my relatives, the Dementieffs traveled from a settlement across the river, where they were living. Grandma Savage had many brothers who shared their carpentry skills with the missionaries in building the mission. Among them was

Mission buildings. Left to right is the church, Father's quarters, round topped building is the "Show hall" where movies and dancing is held. Next is the wood shed and the school. The longer white building with two porches is the mission boys quarters. Next to that is the shop where Dad used to work.

Dad's uncle who we called "Big Uppa". His real name was Ivan Demientieff and what a self made carpenter he was. When we were small children, dad would take us with him when visiting "Big Uppa". He was a kind and gentle man to us small kids, and I never knew he was related to dad until I was much older after "Big Uppa" passed away.

With the help of these men and other villagers, the boys house, (a two story building, downstairs was the recreation room, upstairs the dorm), carpenter shops, church, priest quarters, nuns and girls quarters where the kitchen and dining rooms were located were built. (All beautifully and strongly constructed buildings). With their Russian heritage and carpentry skills Grandma's brothers designed the buildings, especially the church after the Russian art designs. Everything was hand made and showed the builders artistic skills.

For building material, the mission operated a small sawmill which was in operation when I was very young. Later it seemed like the small building sat there unused, due to age of the building and old machinery that didn't work anymore.

The lumber made in the sawmill was used to build the mission buildings and early village houses. The houses of the early village were neatly built in two rows. In front of the back row was a small path that led from one end to the other. There was another walking path by the front row of houses also.

In the front of all the houses was the main dirt road used for trucks or tractors used by the mission or village store keeper.

The typical scenery of every village house was the outhouse located in the back of each home, a garden, a clothes line nearby and a cache for food storage. In the front was a woodpile and wood cutting block. During the winter, sleds were kept in front of or next to the house. Dogs were kept tied next to their own dog houses located in the front of the village, on the river bank for people who lived in the front row of houses. People who had houses in the "back row" tied their dogs in the back of their houses or in front, across the walking path, if there was room.

A little story about outhouses and wood piles. On Halloween, the older boys had fun relocating some of the outhouses and upsetting woodpiles. The day after Halloween, we would see some people moving their outhouses back to place and picking up logs and making their wood piles neat again. Some of the old village men would be pretty angry, grumbling and cussing as they righted what the Halloween pranksters did.

The church was especially beautiful. It's too bad one of the priests in the 1960's took it upon himself to tear the building down without the knowledge of most of the villagers. From what I heard about it, not many knew about the deed until it was well on its way. Later it was found out that the building was eligible to be a historic site. And a beautiful historic site it would have been.

The altar and communion rail inside the church, was carved with designs that were all hand made. There was a loft in the back of the church (with a stairway entrance) where the organ was located for church singing. From the loft there was a small narrow stairway leading to the belfry. A huge bell was located up there with a rope hanging down to the

This is the altar of the church. Grandma Savage's brothers the Demientieff men were part of the carpenters who helped with the building.

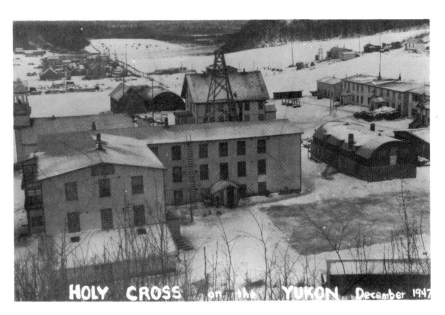

The "L" shaped building is the Sisters and girls living quarters.
The skating rink can be seen in front.

lower floor. The rope was pulled to ring the bell announcing church services and during funeral processions to the cemetery. There was a walkway around the belfry where we would be able to see for miles around.

In the back of the altar, there was a rectory where church supplies were kept. On both sides of the altar there was a door for entry from the rectory to the alter area. This back room was used for priests and alter boys to dress for services.

One morning, as I was attending early mass services, the doors to the back room were both open. Suddenly, as everyone was praying with the priest, the doors slammed shut. This woke everyone up, and we all

The church in Holy Cross. In the summer the trees in front of the church are beautiful with green leaves. This is a winter shot.

wondered if there were spooks playing tricks on us. We never did know what caused both doors to slam shut so suddenly.

There was a story about the church and its haunts. One story I remember well was about one of the boys seeing a "ghost" in the church. Dad told us this story. It seems it was true of one of the boys he grew up with when dad was one of the mission boys. Every morning before the morning church services, one of the boys would be asked to go to the church and start the stove fires. In the basement of the church was a large tank stove. On top of the stove on the floor of the church were open squares with grates to allow the heat to enter the building.

After starting the fire, as the boy started to leave the church, the doors would not open. It seemed as if they were locked. As he struggled to open the doors, he heard a noise at the altar. Looking toward the altar, he saw a priest, who he didn't recognize. The priest told him that he needed an altar boy to help him say mass. The priest said he needed one more mass "that he missed when on earth" in order to be admitted into heaven. So the boy helped, and when the mass was ended the priest disappeared and when the doors were tried again, the boy was able to open them.

Another "ghost" story of the mission happened in the boys dormitory. One day, when holding one of the many fun picnics they held, everyone was in the meadow below the village. A "mission boy" who was ill stayed in bed in the dorm alone. He heard steps walking up the stairs and heard someone coming toward his bed. He saw someone he didn't know, probably Brother Horne, who was said to do many haunts throughout the mission. Anyway this child was so scared, he covered his head with blankets and stayed that way until everyone returned.

A quick explanation of Brother Horne. He was in charge of the many farm animals that were kept in a large barn. Cows, pigs, and even horses were kept there in the late 1800's and early 1900's. When he died, many stories surfaced of his unwanted return.

Every time someone heard an unexplained noise or saw an unwanted shadow, it was usually blamed on Brother Horne.

Sister Mary Pius was another missionary to remember. She was a short, stocky built, stern nun who didn't take nonsense from any of her students. Many of our parents were taught by her when they were children. Sr. Mary Pius taught dad when he was in the 2nd grade. She was my teacher when I was in the fourth or fifth grade. A stricter teacher probably could not be found anywhere in the world. She was not mean, but was so very stern, we couldn't even erase mistakes on our work. We were expected to turn out perfect pages of work without the use of an eraser. I would get so scared of her if I made a mistake and would watch her to make sure she didn't see me erasing. I waited until she was distracted, helping or talking to another student. Then hiding behind the student in front of me I quickly erased my mistakes. Sometime, she would see me and would call sternly, "Dorothy Savage, come here". So shakily, I would walk to her desk, but she usually didn't get angry at me. I would sigh in relief at my good fortune and would make a mental note not to make mistakes again.

When we children were younger, dad sometimes took us to school with the dog team and picked us up after, on cold or stormy days. What fun. Sometimes my cousin, who was a little older than us, would walk us to school and meet us after to take us home. He always had fun things to do on the way home. Sometimes he made us form a train, with him as leader. We all held on as he ran, then he whipped us into the snow alongside of the road. We all took a dive in the deep soft snow laughing and asked for more all the way home.

He was a very special cousin, who was always kind and helpful to us. He protected us from being harassed or beaten by some of the meaner kids in the village. When he was older, he left the village. We missed him a lot, especially when the other kids would fight with us on the way home from school. Our protector was gone.

The sisters/girls house was a big three story "L" shaped building. On one end of the first floor two recreation rooms were located, one for the big girls, and one for little girls.

On the second floor was the younger girls dorm and the third floor was the "big girls" dorm. A huge kitchen with staff dining rooms and pantry were located on the first floor of the other end of the building. The second floor, over the kitchen was the children's dining area with a small chapel on one side and the sisters sleeping/living quarters next to the chapel. Located on the third floor was the work area for sewing, etc., called "Heaven". I remember going to the sisters house on errands for mom. When I asked for one of the sisters, I was told she was up in "Heaven", so I climbed the stairs, located in the central part of the building, to the third floor where "Heaven" was located.

"Heaven" was the sewing area, where the sister in charge and older girls worked daily, sewing mittens, mending clothes and socks for the many mission kids. The room was stocked with cloth, clothes, yarns and skins for sewing.

In the middle of the first floor there was an entry hallway that went past the kitchen, past the recreation areas and around to the recreation/work areas for the nuns. In the middle of that hallway was the infirmary room. It was also used for visitors. If boys were courting girls, this was where they would visit with their chosen one, with one of the nuns sitting in the room as a chaperone. The nun usually sat in one corner of the room doing some kind of work or praying while the young couple visited.

Down the hall from the infirmary were two small rooms where clothes were stored for rummage sales. The village women looked forward to these rummage sales, which supplied everyone with (new) clothes. Mom would come home with a sled or wagon full of clothes in all styles, sizes and colors. Using these she would rip, cut and sew them into new coats, dresses, shirts and blankets for us.

It was fun watching the women in the rummage sale. Everyone would be grabbing clothes, sometimes having a tug of war with the stronger one winning. When we got home with all the things mom bought, we would laugh as we checked the items. Some of the clothes were not something she would buy if she had taken the time to check what she was buying. But the rush of beating each other to the best of the items, sometimes made the women end up with unwanted clothes.

Behind the Sisters' "L" shaped building was a yard used in winter for skating. The priests and older boys worked tirelessly structuring a big skating rink. Some evenings and sometimes Sunday afternoons, the mission would hold skating parties. No one was too cold to skate. The rink was always full of skaters, laughing, chasing or playing tag, all traveling in the same direction around the rink. Even the missionaries joined in on the skating. You could see the Sisters in their long black habits with long heavy coats on, skating among the youngsters. The Sisters would serve hot chocolate to all skaters and spectators.

Another skating area was a small lake located below the village near the hillside. The small slough in front of the village would serve as a skating rink also. In the early days of the mission in the early 1900's, this lake was used for swimming during summer months.

Closer to the bank, in front of the Sisters house, was a small two story building used as the hospital. Mission kids, staff and sometimes villagers who were ill would be kept in the hospital. One of the nuns, who was the nurse, would watch over the patients. On the first floor of the hospital was an examining room, a small kitchen with a huge wood stove, and a small dining room. The second floor had several rooms for patients.

This hospital room was used in the early "Fifties", for a doctor (who was well known in Anchorage) to do his favorite tonsillectomies. He traveled to many villages and removed many tonsils, sometimes needlessly. My two sisters were just a few of his many victims. I remember they had to spend a few days in the mission hospital after their surgery.

Located against the back hill was our schoolhouse. It was a two story building with four classrooms (two downstairs and two upstairs). In the middle of the building was a stairway to get to the two top rooms. Wood was piled in the entryways to the classrooms, to feed the stoves that kept us warm throughout cold winter days. After our long walk to school, we would all stand around the stove to warm up. During the winter, if we reached the mission too early for school, we were allowed to wait in the "Sisters" house. In their main hallway there were two large wood stoves that gave out much needed heat during those cold days. Girls

School house. Two rooms below and two rooms above.
The porch with stairs leads to the top floor.

were allowed to wait there, but boys waited in the boys house recreation room. The heat from the large wood stoves was welcomed after walking in the cold, sometimes up to 50 or 60 below zero. This didn't count the wind chill.

Adjacent to the schoolhouse and sisters house was a large woodshed. This woodshed was piled with logs, and mission boys would be seen daily, cutting wood to feed the many stoves throughout the mission buildings.

The woodshed was kept filled with logs for sawing and chopping. The younger priests and older mission boys traveled by tractor, pulling a large flatbed sled, below the village to cut trees for wood. The main road ran right past in front of our old house area, so when we heard the tractor coming, we would run to the windows to watch them pass by and wave at the workers. Our windows would be frosted over in the cold winter days, so we used our palm to melt spots to see through.

A short story is brought back to me thinking of wood cutting. There was a missionary, "one of the Brother's", who was a little strange to us. He sometimes took walking trips alone, to the woods below the village. We would wave to him as he went by, with no response. Anyway we accepted him as he was. One Saturday, as we were all gathered in the house, the door suddenly flew open and in flew an owl. The door then slammed shut. Excited about the owl, we ran to our "peep" hole in the wall, between the logs, and looking out, we saw the "Brother" walking off. Not a word of explanation from him about the owl. We adopted it and kept it for several weeks, until my parents decided it was well enough to let go. It had a wounded leg or wing, I can't remember which. I remember we kept it tied to our kitchen table leg after it was well, so it wouldn't fly around the house.

Between the shed and sisters house was the "Showhall". The first floor of this round topped two story building was used for storage, and the second floor was used for movies and dancing. After the mission moved away, a small room on the first floor was used for a classroom for the high school age kids. This was where I attended my senior year.

There were not many of us high school students. Less than a dozen I think.

Dad helped with the building of this "showhall" as it was called. He told us the story of how he saw a "ghost' one day. He was working on the first floor of the building alone when he heard noises in the bottom floor, the cellar. From upstairs he looked down to the cellar, thinking one of the missionaries, was there. When he called, no one answered, but he saw a pair of legs walking past the stair area. When one of the priests came by later, dad asked if anyone was in the building with him earlier. The response was that no one was there but dad. So, I guess he saw one of the many haunts that came visiting once in a while.

Chapter 12

In his younger days, dad worked for the mission, doing daily carpentry chores in return for food. This was how I had my first taste of butter. And white butter it was, tasting so good, a welcome change from the daily use of lard (shortening) on bread. He also brought home sugar, flour, salt, tea, coffee, beans, rice and huge cans of some sort of spam. These were welcomed treats for us.

While dad was at the mission working, mom prepared coffee and buttered baking powder biscuits for his coffee breaks. The coffee was mixed with milk and sugar, the way he liked it, and put into a covered mason jar. Carrying the coffee and biscuits, one of us girls delivered it to the shop where dad was working. He was always happy and grateful for these items and would talk to us telling about what he was working on as he ate his snack and drank his coffee. The missionary "Brother" he worked with always had peanuts to share with us during our visits. I could still smell the shop, smelling of wood, machinery and peanuts.

Dad was a pretty good carpenter, expert in making cabinets and shelves, decorated in all sorts of shapes and sizes. In his later years, he made dressers, corner shelves and cupboards to raffle or sell to the villagers for extra money. He made Indian knives which many women liked for fish cutting. His work was outstanding and people still have his hand-crafted items. Dad made small sleds for the smaller kids in our family to ride in. I was always selected to pull a sled load of small boys to church or Sunday movies. What a load. I would be huffing and puffing in the cold winter days pulling that heavy load of small boys.

In later years, living in Anchorage, dad made miniature sleds which he gave to each of his grandsons before he died in 1983. We still have the items as treasured keepsakes.

Mom sewed and knitted for the sisters of the mission for food or clothing. She sewed mittens and mukluks for the mission children. She would knit pairs and pairs of mitten tops, then sewed them to the top of moose skin mittens. When her work was completed, she would send me or one of my sisters to the mission to return the work. The mission sisters gave us food items to take home in exchange, and send more sewing and knitting for mom to do.

On the hillside above the school house was the cemetery. It was fenced in with a wooden rail fence. Higher up the hill above the cemetery was a statue of the blessed virgin Mary. The cemetery was fenced in as a burial place for the baptized catholic people. If anyone died, who was thought to be non catholic, they would be buried outside the fence. At the present time, that practice is not followed. The fence was removed and everyone is buried together with relatives in same areas.

Nuns wearing black long habits with a black veil on their heads were prefects of the girls and were used for teaching in classes. Like I said earlier many of them taught the village people when they were children. Some of the parents grew up as mission kids who were sent there as orphans from villages throughout Alaska. Missionaries traveled from the States and Canada to care for the mission kids and village people.

Dad told us a story about when he first met Sister Ida, who was the cook in the mission, and Sister Kathleen who was my kindergarten teacher. It was called primer class in those days.

One day somewhere in the late 1940's, a plane arrived and landed in the meadow below the village. Since we lived in the cabin at the end of the village, we were closest to the meadow. Dad and a friend ran down to meet the plane. Mom said they thought maybe a friend was returning from working in Flat, Alaska, a small mining town on the Kuskokwin river.

Watching out the window, mom saw dad and the friend walking up the road from the meadow, struggling along, carrying large suitcases. Ahead of them walking were two nuns. They were Sister Ida and Sister

Kathleen, who were both very young and inexperienced with Native people.

They were walking fast ahead of the struggling men, and kept looking back as they walked. Later in years, when the nuns got to know my parents, they shared their story with us that they were scared of the Indian men. They thought the men were wild Indians who would do them harm. Dad laughed and joked with them, saying had he known that, he would have run after them letting out a wild yell. We all laughingly wondered what their reaction would be.

School days were fun. We were taught by the strict, stern nuns, and disrespect, bad behavior, talking back, talking needlessly, fighting, leaving our seats in class was not permitted and not tolerated. Sometimes some of the nuns used to scare me as I thought some of their teaching tactics were a little too strict.

The discipline measures some of the nun teachers took toward some of the students was a little overdone, according to present day standards. I can say their treatment toward some children was pretty harsh. We never dared go home and tell our parents about what happened in class. They supported the nuns and if we dared tell them we were punished in class, then we would be punished again at home.

But there were some nun teachers who were exceptionally kind, gentle and helpful to us small children.

My first school days were fun. Sister Kathleen, my "primer class" teacher, was a kind and gentle teacher with us small children and never a cross word to us escaped her. I looked forward to coming to class and doing the many fun projects she had us do. Some days she read us stories, or had us color pictures. I remember learning the alphabet and numbers.

Thinking back to that time, I can still smell the classroom smell which seemed to be a mixture of crayons, chalk and wood stove smoke. And a warm wood stove it was. A large pot bellied tank stove that gave out welcomed heat after our long walk to school in the cold winter days.

Being the good child that I was, I hardly ever got in trouble and was treated kindly by the nuns. The one time I had punishment, I had to kneel at the back of the room. This was the only time I could remember getting in trouble in class and was very embarrassed. I felt the fault was not even mine, but an accident. I was short so when I was sitting at my desk, my foot barely reached the floor. During class I would swing my foot back and forth on the floor making a little noise. The teacher said to stop, which I did, but forgetting, I absentmindedly continued swinging my feet again. After several reminders, Sister said crossly, "Dorothy Savage, go to the back of the room and kneel on the floor." I did, but never forgot that, as it was pretty embarrassing at that time. I never told my parents about the punishment.

But the missionaries, despite some of their strictness, did do a lot of good for the people. They were sort of our guardian angels making sure people had minimum of health care, food, clothes, education and religion. Even though the nuns were strict, they taught us a lot about self respect and respect for others. Caring for people was their daily chore. I think they sort of raised all the village people, some as small children who lived in the mission until growing up and marrying and moving to their own homes in the village.

Every Christmas the sisters would have entertainment for villagers. A Christmas play was planned with us kids as the entertainers. On the back of the stage platform of the showhall was a trap door used for "us show people" as entrance for our performances. One year my sister and I were used as two blind children singing for the baby Jesus. We knelt on the stage, using dark glasses and sang "Oh Holy Night". This went over well with everyone as we were cheered on and asked for an encore, so we sang again.

Remembering back that far I might as well tell you about my first Christmas play. It was earlier in years, before the show hall was built. The program was held in the girls dorm in the Sisters' house. I think I was in the first grade. My grandmother was sitting in the audience watching, as we wore "Shirley Temple" dresses, singing "Joy To The World", on stage. Now every time I hear that song, I think of my grandmother and can still see her sitting there smilingly watching us, wearing her long black coat and black scarf. That might have been her last Christmas, as she died that next Fall, or sometime close to that time.

Christmas Holidays were such fun days then. Everyone was caught up in the spirit of the holiday, preparing for the week long celebration. For days before the holidays, my cousins would haul water for drinking and fill up our drum tank. Wood would be piled to the ceiling behind the stove in the house. The wooden floors in our cabin were scrubbed with a floor brush and this bar of rough soap. Mom started baking many pies and donuts days before the holiday. Agooduk (Indian ice cream) was made and kept outside frozen.

These activities were done in the late forty's and early fifty's when the mission lived in the village. The preparations took place because of the many fun activities planned for the mission and villagers during "Christmas" week. Every night there was a Christmas play to go to, or a dance, card party, movies, carnival, bingo or potluck. For days before the event, we would practice for our "Holiday Play" that was given for our parents. During school days special time were set aside for practice.

Front row of village houses. The mission is above.

Native dances were provided by the villagers. Dad would do the "Crow" dance accompanied by my sister and myself. Special masks and costumes were made for the dancers to wear. Many days were spent practicing in the home of one of the villagers. It was fun when I attended the practices with dad. My sister and I were the only girls who participated in the dances. When attending practices with dad, we were congratulated by all the older men on our expertise at Native dancing.

I remember one year, the nuns made a special black paint mixture to make my face black like "crows". I thought that was pretty bad stuff to put on, but I always did what I was told to do, so I let them put it on my face. I think the mixture was made out of some kind of face cream dyed with something to turn it black. Anyway when I did the "Crow Dance" the paint on my face took the place of wearing a mask and was more comfortable.

The evening of the native dances, the men gathered behind the stage, which was usually canvas hanging from the ceiling, where they prepared for their individual presentations. Costumes and masks to portray their dances were worn. Such dances as the miner, crow dance, over the mountain, crane dance, etc. were done. This was so much fun. The older men knew the language and were able to sing in their loud voices accompanied by a drum. The drum was a piece of skin in a tight round frame. A narrow wooden stick was used to beat on it to make the loud sound. Once in a while the drums had to be rubbed with water to keep it from drying out. Their singing would be accompanied with arguments sometimes when one would think the other wasn't singing the right way. But the arguments were usually forgotten when it was time for the next dance and song.

In days before Christmas, and in some evenings we would join with the Sisters to make wreaths out of pine tree branches to decorate the church. The church looked so beautiful and smelled like pine with all the tree decorations. There was a life sized manger of the nativity scene near the alter. All the various holiday preparations were done under the directions of the nuns.

Midnight mass on Christmas Eve was attended by the whole village. This was a special time for everyone. We all dressed in new clothes that our mom labored over for hours sewing for us. Everyone had new mukluks, knitted socks, new scarves, gloves, overcoats and dresses. I enjoyed sitting in church watching villagers come to church on Christmas Eve and would compare what everyone was wearing "new".

Midnight mass was so beautifully done by several of the priests, with alter boys in attendance. A piano or organ was located in the loft at the back of the church played by one of the nuns. Everyone joined in loudly singing different songs during the mass, despite women and girls sitting to one side and men and boys the other side.

When we were living in our old house at the end of the village, dad would harness the dogs, cover the sled with canvas tarp, put blankets on top of that for us to sit in and we would all ride to attend midnight mass. It was fun riding in the sled at night over the snow packed road. Other times it would be snowing and the stillness at night with the falling snow was breathless. On clear cold nights the stars were all out and the moon would be brightly shining, it was truly a "Silent Night, Holy Night".

When we reached the mission, where the church was located, there would be other dog teams tied around the mission yard, and in the wood shed. This was like a parking lot of cars, only instead, we had dog teams. The dogs would lay on the ground, curled up together keeping warm waiting for us.

The "mission kids" all filed into the church in a line. Boys to one side, girls to the other side. Even the village people were separated. Men and boys on one side, women and girls to the other side. When it was time to receive communion, we all filed up to the alter and knelt at the communion rail separated again. I'm not sure of the purpose of the segregation, and no one complained about it but accepted the "separation" rule without complaints.

After midnight mass we went home to have snacks of donuts, pies, salmon strips, or native ice cream and tea. Sometimes dad would get out his frozen fish for us to share with him, against mom's approval.

On Christmas Eve we were so anxious for "Santa" to arrive. Somehow my parents managed to have a present for everyone of us many kids. They prepared us for Santas' arrival by telling us we had to stay in the back room until he arrived. When Santa arrived, we were so excited about seeing him in his red suit, white beard, fat belly and jolly laugh. He always gave mom a kiss. It was a little suspicious that dad always happened to be gone when Santa arrived. His explanation was that he was out looking for Santa and returning dad would say "darn it, I missed Santa again". We excitedly told him all about the visit and that Santa stole a kiss from mom. Later when we were older we sort of put two and two together and figured out who the "real Santa" was. My auntie lived up the rode and her house was used for dad's change into the red suit costume. What fun it was to see Jolly Old St. Nick, until we figured out who he really was.

On Christmas day, in the afternoon, there was a celebration called "Christmas Tree", held in the "show hall" or village hall. Everyone attended. greeting "Santa" with his many bags of toys and candy and singing "Jingle Bells". The Sisters' popcorn balls were one of the main stocking stuffers given to us by "Santa". It seems like everyone received a gift of some sort.

Then everyone went home to have their Christmas dinner of moose or turkey. In the evening the mission provided us with a movie for the culmination of the days celebration. What happy times these were for everyone.

Alcohol was present but at a minimum during this time of my childhood. We hardly saw anyone walking around during the day involved with alcohol. It was present but not as rampant, open and out of control as it is now. If intoxicated people were seen in public they were discouraged by the village council men. There were a few who joined the activities, but if they got out of hand or looked as if they were overindulging they were "kicked" out by the priests or councilmen. We never heard of drugs. The closest to drugs would probably be smoking a cigarette occasionally. Teens were never seen under the "influence" and it was unheard of in younger kids. Bad language was hardly ever heard from our young mouths.

This is my opinion of the rampancy and abuse of alcohol in villages. It's happening all over the State. I feel it's the responsibility of parents to teach their children at young ages to respect themselves and stay away from alcohol and drugs. We need to teach our children to be strong in making good choices. Parents can do this by using themselves as an example and not use alcohol and drugs themselves. If this is done, children will not be dependent on it and therefore future generations will not look to alcohol and drugs as a way of having so called "fun" or an escape from being bored. There is nothing about alcohol and drugs that's fun. It brings misery, depression, sickness, unhappiness, unnecessary deaths to our people. Fun can be other things such as hunting, fishing, traveling in the wilderness with our families. In the village community activities can be started to interest children in leading a clean life. Elders can have weekly meetings to advising and encouraging children on how to stay away from alcohol and drugs. These elders have to believe in what they are doing and have to set an example by staying away from these bad habits also. Parents do not need to share drinks and drugs with their children. Some think it's a way of letting children think they care for them. Not true. Sharing drinks and drugs with your children is just as good as murder.

As for "bootleggers". They are responsible for every alcohol related deaths in the village where they sell drinks. They might say the people are stupid and can't handle the drinks. If that's so then they, as selling the "booze" are responsible for the people they are selling to. If there is a suicide or other deaths from the alcohol, the bootlegger is just as good as a murderer. He/she might as well have given the loaded gun to the person committing the suicide. They might as well have put the person in a boat and pushed them overboard, or left them outside in cold winter temperatures to freeze.

Village people can fight bootleggers by having zero tolerance. Whether friend or relative, remove the bootlegger from the village without feeling guilty or afraid of angry relatives. I would rather have

115

people angry at me knowing that I removed a bootlegger from the village and saved a young persons life. If you know of bootleggers and drug sellers, report them to authorities instead of saying it's none of your business. It is our business and responsibility to keep young people safe, alive and happy.

Now that I've gotten this off of my mind, I'll continue with my story.

Chapter 13

In January or February we sometimes had a "Potlatch". A potlatch was a celebration given in honor of people within a village or between villages or to honor the dead. For instance a village could give a potlatch and invite another village as guests, or within a village men would give a potlatch for women or the other way around. All participants chose a "Partner" who they would be responsible for. The "Partner" would be given meals throughout the day. Gifts and more food were passed around during the evening celebrations of native dancing. If you had a "Partner" you would be responsible for fixing a dish of food for them and passing out gifts. Things given as gifts were socks, cigarettes, candy, gum, scarves, clothes, gloves, bullets, crackers and smoked fish.

In Holy Cross, I remember we had two potlatches. One was given by the men for women. My "Partner" was Victor Woods who was married to my favorite grandma, Erena. I was invited to their house for meals, and was given gifts and food at the evening events.

The potlatch lasted for about three days. The culmination was an Indian Dance in the village hall. If the men were giving the potlatch, they would do the entertainment. A year or later the women gave their pay back potlatch for men.

Other potlatches given were for funerals and for past deaths. This practice was not done in Holy Cross, but followed in other surrounding villages.

For burials, food was prepared and shared by everyone in the community hall. The deceased always had a plate of food fixed for them before everyone ate. A glass of water and cup of tea or coffee was placed by the coffin along with the food. The food which was changed for each meal, was kept in a bag and later burned during the funeral.

Deceased people were dressed in the finest clothes made by local women. Mukluks, fur parkas, beaded belts, mittens and fur hats were made. Local women and even others from surrounding villages gathered together and helped to sew for days before the funeral. Food preparations were done by other people. Men and boys were involved in digging the grave, moose hunting, making a cross and cover for the casket. The whole village was busy with the activities. Grief for the loss of the loved one was put aside temporarily when funeral preparations had to be done. This was part of the healing and acceptance process.

When there was a death in the village, coffins were built by village men. Dad was usually the carpenter in charge of this. He made many coffins for many people in his lifetime, until the commercial type coffins came to use. Commercial coffins were ordered from Anchorage and are delivered priority by local airlines. Homemade coffins were used in the early days until about the late 1960's.

Mom still follows the burial process done by people in her village when she was growing up. She carefully explains to us the steps they took when caring for their deceased.

Small gifts were given to put in the coffin of the deceased. A cloth traveling bag was prepared with matches, cigarettes (if they smoked), scissors, needles, thread and anything we thought they would need traveling on their last journey.

Mom said the traveling took four days. Thus, four candles were put in the coffin, one on each corner to light the way of the traveler. Sometimes a favorite hunting gun was sent with the deceased.

The evening before the burial, a potluck was held in the village hall. Everyone gathered there to share a last meal with their loved one. At the potluck, food is brought in the village hall by everyone. Before everyone started the meal, a plate was fixed for the deceased with a small portion from everything brought in to eat. Coffee or tea was placed by the coffin with the food. The village hall would be filled with people, both from the village and surrounding villages, who traveled to attend the funeral, giving their support and condolences to families and to participate in the burial activities.

Native songs would be shared and on the morning of the burial a farewell song would be performed. A few people in mom's village know how to do the farewell song which is a very special and touching performance.

When the coffin is removed from the hall and brought to church for the funeral, three rocks are placed in the hall on the place where the coffin was. These rocks were to be kept there for a day to ensure that the spirit of the deceased was sent off safely on their journey.

Another event done for deceased people was a potlatch, called a "parky feast", given usually a year or two after the death. The potlatch was given by a relative of the deceased. A person was chosen to portray the dead person and clothes and gifts were prepared for that person. Again mukluks, hats, parkas, mittens were made. Food was prepared and served the evening of the event. The chosen person was dressed in the prepared clothing, gifts were presented and food was served to the person by the family of the deceased.

After gifts were given the family of the deceased gathered together to say farewell to the person representing their dead loved one. Then the chosen person had to leave the village hall and walk toward the cemetery and return back. This is a strict event where the person was not allowed to look around. Stories are that if that person looked elsewhere there was a possibility of something bad happening. Sometimes they would see the person they represented or other "things" would happen.

Upon the return from the walk to the cemetery, there would be "native" dances given by the family. Other villagers would join in and it would turn out to be a fun event of native dancing, singing, eating and gift giving. There would be lots of delicious native foods, pots of moose meat and fish prepared in all styles. Tables would be laden down with side dishes of salads, vegetables, Indian ice creams of all kinds, with blueberries, salmon berries and even raisins. Salmon strips and other smoked fish would be plentiful along with many dishes of dessert. What a bountiful table the villagers turned out.

A January event was the yearly winter carnival. Dog races were held by local people. There were races for kids, boys and older men, some for girls and women.

When I was about sixteen years old I raced in the girls race. I had three or four dogs and the race was about two miles around the old garden area up the mission way and back to the start point by the main road. My dogs were going so fast I could hardly hold on, so half way around, I climbed into the sled. When I was coming to the finish line I climbed out of the sled to the back, but fell off. I jumped up and started running after the sled and dogs trying to catch up before they reached the finish line. It's a good thing some of the men on the side line grabbed my sled and held onto it until I caught up. I was so happy to reach the finish line, together with my dogs and sled, but promised myself never to race again. My reward was winning third place with a prize of fifty cents.

Events, such as gunny sack races, nail hammering, etc. were done. One year in the nail hammering event for women, mom entered the contest. Guess who won that one, yes mom did. We told her the many hours she spent at home hammering nails making cupboards and room partitions paid off. Her prize with a sack of flour.

Before carnivals were held, money for prizes was raised by having bake sale dances.

The whole village contributed to these events.

At the time the missionaries were living in the village, they had carnivals during winter months in the missions buildings and sometimes outside during the month of May. On Halloween, we had a carnival, with a "witch", her broom and cat in attendance. These carnivals were fun, with many games, prizes and apple bobbing. We enjoyed the mission Sister's delicious popcorn balls. I was always so afraid of the witch until I found out it was one of the sisters or bigger girls of the mission.

Celebrating weddings was always special in the village. First, three wedding announcements, called banns, had to be made in the church during Sunday mass.

The day of the wedding, the whole village gathered in the church to watch the young people joined together in holy matrimony. The small church would be packed from front to back with all the village people.

After the wedding mass, the whole village was invited to participate in a feast given by the parents of the married couple. It was usually given by the parents of the groom. Everyone visited the home of the groom during the day for a meal prepared by the parents. Gifts and congratulations were given to the married folks.

Village men gunny sack race during one of the carnivals the mission held. The house is quarters for priests, brothers and scholastics.

In the evening a dance was held in their honor. Everyone in the village attended, dancing into the early hours of the next morning. What a celebration these weddings were. It was sort of a holiday for everyone.

In the late 1940's and on I remember women having their babies at home. Of the fifteen children mom had, all were delivered at home, fishcamp or trapping camp, except for the last who was born in the hospital at Bethel, Alaska. My oldest sister was born while mom and dad were living in the trapline located up the Innoko river.

At that time, my parents traveled with grandparents to that area to spend the winter trapping. Here they settled and build small log cabins to live in. When it was time, my sister was delivered by grandma and aunts.

Another sister was delivered across the village in the point at a small camp they lived in at that time. Then there were others delivered at fishcamp also.

In the village babies were delivered by the older "experienced" women. When it came time for baby delivery, these women would be sent for to spend several long hours, sometimes all night vigils, waiting to welcome the new arrivals.

After births, baptism was always eminent. The missionaries saw to it that all us newborn babies were properly christened with the name of a saint. We had godparents who were chosen by our parents, either relatives or friends in the village.

During the windy month of March, when the mission was still in the village, a retreat would be held for everyone. When the retreat was held, we had to keep silent, without talking to each other, for the whole day. I used to be so scared to make a sound even, during these retreats. There was a church service held about three times a day, which all the retreaters attended. Everyone would participate, praying and listening to the priests' sermons. Then we returned home to live our lives in silence. The retreats lasted about three days. What a relief it was when that ended and it seemed like we couldn't talk enough after the days of silence.

Even though it was windy and cold at times, village people accepted and ignored the weather to attend church services. We all bundled up in our warmest clothes and sometimes fighting the strong winds or blowing snows, would walk to the mission to attend services.

When I was in the eighth grade, a retreat was held for us eighth graders. We were invited to spend three days in the mission (old boys house). During this time we ate, worked, attended sermons and prayer services all in silence. I remember living in the room with several other girls my age and a teacher who was our chaperone. We all had our chores to do such as cooking, doing dishes, sweeping floors, etc. This was sort of fun, but I wanted to be home. I was happy when the retreat ended and was able to return home to my family who lived only about a two minute walk from where we were.

The month of March was windy and cold. Sometimes so windy that we would open our coats to use like a sail and let the wind blow us along, running down the road.

Sometimes during the months of January or February, we would get a big thaw where temperatures would rise for a few days. Then the weather turned cold and the snow would be like ice making it possible to walk on top without sinking. This was fun, especially for us being able to run in the woods between trees and everywhere.

Chapter 14

With the coming of "Spring" it was time for beaver trapping. This event took place during the month of March. Men and boys took this event seriously as it was the last money making chance for them until fishing time. That is beside muskrat hunting, but we'll talk about that a little later. Beaver trappers usually traveled to their trapline by dog sleds, but others would have an airplane drop them off. Trappers stayed out in their camp for about a month.

To go to his trapline, dad always traveled by dog sled. He prepared for days, the same as he did in the Fall for other fur trapping. The sled was brought in the house to thaw out so mending could be done. Broken parts were replaced, runners and brakes checked. New dog harnesses were sewn, old ones mended. Mom sewed many small dog booties to protect the dog feet against cuts from the Spring ice.

When beaver trapping season ended, dad returned home, sometimes with many beaver pelts. These were dried on racks stacked outside against the house. The Spring sun was getting warmer, so that helped with the drying. Beaver meat was plentiful and we had it for many meals. Beaver was not one of my favorite foods, as like bear meat it was fatty and oily. Some people loved the beaver tail when baked or boiled.

The faces of the trappers, when they returned from trapping, were wind worn and sun burned from being out in the weather. But they were all happy to be back to the village with their families again.

Another Spring money making event was muskrat hunting. Many of the men and boys traveled to the small lakes for this event. Some stayed only a day, others camped out for several days, but always had a few skins when returning.

One year when I was about eight or nine years old my parents moved us to "Spring Camp" for muskrat hunting. It was about the middle of April when we moved there. The camp was located in a slough about twenty miles below the village.

Before the final move, dad traveled with relatives, by dog sled to prepare the camp. Tents were put up and made ready for our arrival. Our small boat and canoe were also brought to the camp, pulled by dog sled.

When moving day came, we were taken to the camp by airplane, which took about two or three trips. When we landed at the camp, in the middle of nowhere, it was all winter with lots of snow and everything looked so lonely and isolated. The tent was a welcome site, with spruce branches placed on the floor for us to put our bedding on. Fire was started in the small Yukon stove that was previously installed. Soon the welcome warmth was felt by all.

The stove was great, as it warmed up the tent fast. Dad kept the stove going all night to keep us warm while sleeping. I didn't know it then, but later in years past, mom said dad would get up several times during the night to stoke the fire and keep it just warm enough to keep the cold out and away from us.

Getting used to the camp was easy as we had many events to keep us busy. We settled in and everyday chores were routine. Melted snow or ice was used for water. Food was provided by hunting for moose and the muskrat caught for fur.

The meat of the muskrat was dried and later cooked for meals. Hunting took place daily by dad and others who were with us. My cousin and her husband lived in the camp with us. Everyday the men searched for muskrats in small surrounding lakes. When caught, the fur was skinned out of the body and stretched in a metal frame stretcher, and left to dry.

The fur was stored and saved for use when returning to the village. It would be traded in the local store for food and money. A few times, dad made a day trip to the village to trade some of the fur and replenish our food supply. He would return with special treats for us.

For entertainment I remember listening to my cousins' husband and his brother playing the guitar and singing "Hank Williams" songs.

126

That was the first time I could remember hearing Hank Williams songs, which I grew to like. Later I heard them on the radio and recognized the songs from the singing I heard in camp.

Other entertainment for us kids was playing tag in the snow on the side of the slough. The snow was deep so we made trails to play in. We had fun running in the snow, rolling down the small banks.

Sledding was a winter entertainment in camp, as well as in the village. We sledded down the river bank using card board paper in place of sleds.

In the village we were allowed to sled down the bank in front of our old house area. If we had no sleds, again card board paper was used to slide with. Sometimes we made skis out of barrel sides with a piece of leather nailed to the middle for our feet to fit in. At times, our friends allowed us to join them on their toboggan. We would slide down the hill together to the bottom and rolled in the snow, laughing and yelling when we hit the snow banks.

When mom didn't want us staying out after dark she told us the following legend story. She said if we slide down the bank or hill after dark an old woman would open her mouth at the bottom of the bank and swallow us. We believed her and never stayed out after dark. When my own children were growing up in the city, they went sledding a lot. Not wanting them out after dark, I would tell them this story. I never knew it then, but they believed my story and never stayed out after dark. Recently my youngest son told me they believed my myth and actually thought they would get swallowed by this mysterious old woman if sledding after dark. He said his brother would say, "it's getting dark, we better go home so the old woman wouldn't swallow us" and they would promptly come home.

Other entertainment in Spring camp when the snow was gone, was playing in the woods. Pretending to be king or queen we made a throne out of moss and sat on it to be the ruler. We also made small play stoves out of empty milk cans with a piece of cast iron sheet for the top. A small fire was made under that and we prepared our pretend food. This was done in the camp where the ground was safe for building fire.

The weather stayed pretty good, but sometimes we had snowstorms during the early Spring. Later when it was warmer, snow melted, but we would be hit by sudden rain or hail storms. I remember we had to run into the tent when this happened, as we spent a lot of our time playing outdoors. When the hail hit, we could hear the large pellets falling against the top of the tent. Then all of a sudden all was well, the sun would appear again and we would all run out of the tent to resume our activities. What fun days.

At the bottom of the slough a small stream of water was running. This stream grew daily as the weather got warmer with the Spring sun. Soon the snow was all gone, everything seemed to be changing and the slough snow and ice was all gone.

Suddenly, leaves sprang out of tree branches, grass was popping out of the ground, and ducks and geese were coming in from their long winter journey. The ice on the main river was breaking up. At breakup you could hear the noise of the large chunks of ice breaking and piling up on each other.

The slough water started rising, so we had to relocate our camp to higher ground. Using the small boat we had, dad checked the surrounding areas until he found the right place. All our belongings were then moved by boat, to the new location and we once again settled in.

Another food subsistence activity in the camp, was dipping for fish in the slough. We all attended this activity, but only the older men and mom got to do the dipping. We were not allowed to be near the bank for safety reasons. Pike and white fish were caught. This was a welcome change to our daily diet of muskrat, geese and ducks.

One day, while the men were out muskrat hunting, mom walked to the bank of the slough and looking in the water, she saw many fish swimming. Excitedly returning to the tent, she dug in the storage boxes for the small fishnet made for dipping. Willows were cut, and made into a round top to tie the fishnet to. A long wooden pole was then attached to the round fishnet frame. Using this she returned to the slough and dipped for the fish. Surprisingly, her first dip brought in the net filled with small white fish.

Mom was so excited for her good catch. Returning to camp, she scraped the scales off the skin, cleaned the fish, cut them and made hanging poles for drying and smoking.

Dad and his hunting companions returned to camp during the night, and mom could hear them talking outside the tent. Dad was expressing his surprise to the others about the many fish hanging. They were wondering out loud where all that fish came from. They figured out it was mom's work. Coming into the tent, dad congratulated her on her expertise at fishing and making a dip net.

Sometimes, my parents took us with them to hunt for geese and ducks. We all walked to the main river area where there were large sandbars. Dad made model geese and ducks out of mud. Then we all hid in the nearby woods and mimicked the calling of the geese. When they landed to investigate the dummy birds and hearing our calls, dad and the other men would start shooting. Soon we had a large flock of dead fowl to tend to. The plucking of feathers took place, an unfun activity. At that time I was a little too young, so got out of doing that chore. The soup and roast made of these birds was a delicious addition to our daily diet of fish and muskrat.

Then one day, in the warm sunny days of May, a boat came for us to move back to Holy Cross. Everything was packed and ready for the trip. Dads uncle came for us for the move. The trip to Holy Cross took all day, as the engine must have been something like three or four horse power. The distance to the village was only about twenty miles, but it took so long we stopped on the way for a lunch/rest break.

It was always nice to be back in the village after living in camp isolation for so long. Actually it was probably only about a month that we stayed away, but it seemed longer.

Back in the village we returned to school and waited for the end of the school year. During school we worked hard in class, but playtime was fun. At recess, we rushed outside to play games such as hopscotch, marbles, Eskimo baseball or plain baseball. All of us who participated in playing marbles had a pocket full of marbles with one as a special "Shooter". For hopscotch, we also had a special piece of glass in our pockets, that we used for throwing to the hopscotch blocks. We didn't have "duties" to keep us under control during recess. It seems like we were so busy having fun with these simple games, none of us had time to have arguments or fights. If we did we resolved it ourselves. We usually ignored the trouble makers.

Bathroom breaks were taken during recess. There were two large outhouses, one for boys located closer to the boys house, the other for girls was located on the hillside near the girls/sisters house. The outhouses were long buildings with about ten "stalls" side by side with doors. It was no fun using these outhouses on cold days. We had no toilet paper so Sears catalogs were put to good use.

When my older cousins left the village, we girls had to do the chores they did. We learned to saw and cut wood, which was an everyday chore, along with carrying water. When the mission was in the village, school was let out at lunch time to about 3:30 p.m. for people to do chores before the dark settled in.

We would hitch up the dog team, load our gas cans into the sled and travel to the water hole in the back of the village, around the hill. A well used trail was made during winter from all the dog sled trips to the water hole. There was a small lake we had to cross and sometimes we would meet friends there to race our dog sleds across this lake. At times returning with full water cans we would have a mishap and tip the sled over. Spilling all the water, we would then have to return to the water hole to refill. This took us longer to return home. Our parents would be a little worried and upset that we took so long. We usually blamed our delay on the "lazy" dogs that didn't want to run fast. We never told them about our racing activities on the small lake.

The new house, dad built, was located above the mission area near the hillside. During winter when wood was scarce, my cousin and I would climb the hill in the back of the house carrying a saw to cut several birch trees. We had to drag the logs down hill through deep snow and with cold weather at times. Reaching the house we would warm up for a bit, then return outside to saw the birch into pieces and chop these into smaller pieces to fit into the stove.

It seemed like every Spring breakup we would have river floods. When my family lived at the end of the village in our old house, we had to move to temporary quarters, on higher grounds because of flooding. We stayed in a tent, or sometimes, we stayed in the village hall, sharing space with other flood stricken families.

During floods, school would be let out for a few days. It seemed like a holiday. People helped each other move, using boats to travel between homes. The floods hit only houses in the lower half of the village where grounds were lower. Before floods, when break up happened, ice would be flowing by. People could tell the river was rising by using a measuring stick close to the shore. Watching was done carefully to ensure that people had enough time to move out of their homes. Also, belongings had to be moved higher in homes to ensure that they stayed dry if the water should reach the houses.

Floods were caused when the flowing ice jammed below the village. The usual jam location was where the Yukon river turned in a curve. The ice would pile up, causing the water to backup and cause floods to grounds above the jam area.

Sometimes a military helicopter would be sent to bomb the jam. This was an exciting time for everyone. If school was in session, we would be let out. Many of us would climb the hill in the back of the village to watch the bombing. After that the water would recede and we were able to move back to our homes to salvage what we could and do the clean-up job. Mud was pretty hard to clean off of floors and walls.

Every Spring the missionaries set aside a day for everyone to do yard work. Raking all the winter trash was a chore everyone participated in. Our family worked all day, cleaning the yard, garden and dog areas. Under the "Cache" was mucked out and all the trash was piled in an old wagon and taken to the dump site. The dump site was down the road from our house, where a small slough was located with a wooden bridge over it.

In the evening, when we were done with the cleaning, the missionaries sometimes rewarded everyone for their hard days work by showing a movie, after the benediction that was held in the church.

Being a catholic village, there were many religious activities throughout the year.

My favorite to remember was during the Month of May, which was set aside to honor the blessed virgin. This ceremony was done in the, early 1950's. Each evening we had the rosary said in a different village family house. Everyone would gather in that house with the priest or nuns to say the rosary and sing songs. People had a statue of the blessed virgin in their house in a special corner. It would be decorated with pretty cloth and fresh spring plants or flowers.

The culmination of this celebration would be to have benediction one evening and a procession up the mountain to the statue of the blessed virgin. Everyone in the village participated, reciting prayers and singing songs while walking in the procession. When we reached the blessed virgin's statue,we all gathered around for more prayer. The statue was located on the hillside, above the cemetery, reached by an old horse trail in the back of the mountain. The statue is still standing as it was many years ago.

The mission closed in 1956. A new school was built near Glenallen called Copper Valley school. On October 13, 1956, a cold day, the mission kids were flown by Alaska Airlines to Aniak. The moving event was called "Operation Snowbird". There were three, five passenger planes that flew the kids trip after trip to Aniak. In Aniak a DC 4 was waiting to take the kids and missionaries to Gulkana where they were bused to the new school site located below Glenallen, Alaska.

My sister was one of the kids who were first moved to the new school. She was a freshman in high school at that time.

The village people were all sad to see the missionaries leave. They were always there for us throughout all of our growing up days, even the older people. Now they were gone and it seemed lonely and bleak without seeing the busy activities in the mission area. The buildings looked empty and abandoned.

Some of the missionaries were left behind, but it was never the same.

Chapter 15

When we girls were younger children, in the late 1940's and early 1950's dad would leave town to do river boat piloting during summer months. This was usually from late April until late August. He traveled to Nenana and worked the whole summer piloting boats, delivering supplies to surrounding villages. It was fun when he returned, with gifts and candy for us. For several years he left home during summer months to do river boat piloting.

It was only when he stopped doing the river boat work that we returned to reopening our "Fishcamp" during summer months.

In the Spring of 1951, we all moved to Fairbanks to live with dads cousin who had a river boat freighting business. This was in mid or late April. Dad worked for him during that Spring, repairing boats and barges preparing them for freighting during the summer. When the freighting season was ready, we all moved to Nenana by boat to spend the summer there, while dad traveled down the river piloting the freight boat.

Living in Nenana that summer was an experience not lightly forgotten. Everything was different. The house we lived in was a two bedroom building. It was at the end of the street near the wooded area. The other side of the wooded area was the railroad tracks. Every evening we heard the train coming by as it stopped at the depot before continuing to Fairbanks.

The kids in our family were not real happy about being away from home and relatives. I was so lonesome for Holy Cross, I sometimes, would wake up and think I was home again. Sometimes, I dreamed I was home.

Finally, after listening to all our complaints about homesickness, dad decided to move us back to the village.

It was sometime in mid August that we packed everything and boarded the river boat. We traveled down the Yukon River passing several villages until we reached Galena. On the way we passed the villages of Minto, Tanana, Ruby and then Galena. I was about nine years old, but remember briefly some of the villages.

We stayed in Galena a few days, or weeks, while dad went delivering freight with the boat. When he returned, we boarded the boat again and continued on the journey home. We traveled to Kaltag, Koyukuk and finally Nulato. In Nulato we stayed with an old lady who was said to be a relative, but I'm still not sure of that relationship. Anyway, she was very kind to us and welcomed us to her home. Later on I heard she was tired of us lively children under foot and told a local pilot to take us back to Holy Cross.

Finally dad returned from supply delivery and announced it was time for us to make our final journey home to Holy Cross. On the day to travel, we walked up to the airfield, which was located on a mountain top. The first day, my two older cousins, older sisters and I were taken by bush plane, home at last.

Reaching the village, we were so happy and excited. We first went to our auntie Martha's house. Being dad's only sister, she welcomed us warmly with hugs and signs of welcome and fed us bread and fish, washed down with the ever popular tea.

A little about my auntie Martha. She lived in her small log cabin a little ways above our house at the end of the village. I loved to visit her and watch her sewing or knitting. She was a deaf mute, so she didn't talk, but made signs, which we all understood. When visiting her she would give me brown sugar candy or biscuits, just like grandma used to do.

Sometimes, she would be rolling yarn into a ball from the yarn skeins she had. She would have me sit on the floor in front of her and hold the long yarn skein between my hands and she would roll it into a ball. I was always fascinated by the speed she rolled the yarn and enjoyed helping and watching her do that job.

Speaking of the speed in which she worked, Auntie Martha was able to knit a pair of gloves or socks in a day. Her sewing also was done with speed, but was beautifully, artfully and carefully done.

I remember her neatly kept cabin, with all her belongings placed in carefully chosen places. One thing I always remembered was her cloth sewing kit hanging on the wall by her bed. The sewing kit always fascinated me, when I saw how neatly it was made. I would have liked to have had it, but after she died the local village women were able, with her husbands permission, to claim all her belongings. Dad was working as a river boat pilot at that time and was not home. If he had been home, I'm sure we would have been able to have at least one souvenir of her life with us.

Continuing on our return to the village, after our greetings with auntie, we went running up the road to the village to visit long missed friends. We received warm hugs of welcome from some of the older people whose kids were friends of my sisters.

The next day, mom and the rest of the siblings arrived by the same bush plane. We all moved back into our small log cabin to get settled in and wait for dad's arrival when summer boating was done. It was great to be home again with all our relatives and friends.

We soon settled in to the routine of living in our village again and soon school opened and we were able to forget the lonesomeness we experienced away from home that summer.

Chapter 16

Across from Holy Cross in the slough that led to the Innoko river was another smaller slough that led another direction from the Innoko river. We sometimes traveled in this slough to pick raspberries. The large, delicious berries were in abundance in some areas along the banks of the slough. I think we picked as many berries as we ate. One berry in the bucket, the next in our mouth, until we filled our buckets full of the red delicious berries and sometimes got a stomach ache from eating as much as we picked. When we returned back to Holy Cross, mom made jam out of the berries we picked.

Along this same slough, there was a small camp where this old German or French man lived. I guessed he was either German or French from the accent he had. Ed Blank was what he was called. I think he was named that, because he didn't have a last name when he first came there, so people gave him the last name of "Blank". The story about Ed Blank was that he escaped from some foreign country because he didn't want to be forced into military service there.

He lived in his camp year round alone, with his dog, garden, and in his small cabin with many stuffed wild animals and fowl. I remember seeing a stuffed owl. He also had many beautifully painted decorated egg shells threaded together in a long row and hanging on the walls. This was probably how he passed the lonely days he spent alone in camp.

On our raspberry picking trips, we usually stopped at his camp for a visit. We were always welcomed by him and his small barking dog. One of my favorite memories of him was this great big pot of stew he always seemed to have. He fed all of us with the delicious stew and home made bread. Mom said he was serving her and dad tea at one visit. Having only one cup for dad, Mr. Blank, reached under the table on the floor and picked up a cup he found. It had a lot of dust in it, but he proceeded to pour tea into it and gave it to mom. Not wanting to be rude, she didn't say anything, but accepted the tea and drank it, worrying silently about the dust in it.

What a gardener he was with a garden filled with huge vegetables, heads of cabbages, carrots and potatoes. He told mom and dad he boiled fish and used the broth from that as fertilizer for his garden. He poured some of the broth in the ground along with a potato before covering it up. This served as a healthy fertilizer and seemed to work as his garden produced huge vegetables and in abundance.

Living in the slough yearly, he made occasional trips to the village. Everyone welcomed him to visit and sometimes he would stay in our house during some of his visits.

I remember one funny story about this old gentle fellow. One Christmas season, while visiting Holy Cross, he spent some time in our house sharing homebrew with dad. After several bottles of the stuff, he decided he needed to visit the outhouse. In front of our door there was a small bank. It was a small sloped hill about ten feet high and in December there was a lot of snow. Anyway, after leaving the house, he didn't return, so dad told us to look for him. Out the door we went to hear his cries for help. When we looked where the voice was coming from, he was at the bottom of the snowy bank trying to crawl up toward our house. He was all full of snow, and we found out that he missed the path to the outhouse and rolled over the bank instead. What a funny site it was to see him at the bottom trying to crawl up in the snow. The happy ending was that we pulled him up the bank and returned him to the house to shake off the snow and warm him by the stove. Everyone laughed and teased him about rolling under the bank. He pretended to be angry, swearing about it, but eventually saw the humor of it.

When I was finished with the eighth grade, at the age of thirteen, I traveled to the new mission school located near Copper Center, Alaska called Copper Valley School. Several other boys and girls from the village were with me. We flew by mail plane to McGrath and traveled from there by Alaska Airlines in a larger plane to Anchorage. In

Anchorage, missionaries met us and took care of us until we were able to travel by car to the school located not far from Glenallen, Alaska.

This was the first time I was introduced to the "television". What an interesting thing that was and fun to watch even though it was black and white. In the village we didn't have television but watched movies weekly in the village hall. Radios were used and often we listened to stories such as the "Lone Ranger", Cinderella" and some detective story call "The Shadow".

I stayed at the school for my freshman year. That was one of the longest, hardest years I could remember. Homesickness was rampant throughout the school. Sniffles and crying could be heard throughout the dorm at bedtime when the lights were turned out.

I remember being awakened on Saturday mornings by this loud marching music played on the record player by the "Sister" who was in charge of us. If this wasn't successful in getting us out of bed, she would walk by our beds or rooms clapping her hands and saying "get up girls" all the way down the hall. To this day whenever I hear marching music, it brings those memories back to me.

At the end of the year, when school was out, we all returned to our village for the summer.

I stayed in the village for the next few years, alternating with skipping a year of school to help my parents at home or attending the small high school there. Finally I somehow reached my junior year. One Spring day in the middle of April in 1961, when I was a junior in high school, I left the village for Fairbanks.

This journey was unexpected. On that particular day, I attended the morning session of school until the midday lunch break. When I returned home for lunch, dad came home from the village and told me that a priest "Father Woods" had arrived from McGrath. Father Woods wanted to know if I was interested in traveling with him in his small "Cessna", with him as the pilot, to McGrath and work for a family there. If I was interested, I had to be ready to travel by 4:00 p.m. that day.

I didn't have to think of an answer very long. It was a big "YES". Returning to school that day was out of my mind, as I packed my few clothes as fast as I could. I was ready long before 4:00 p.m.

At departure time, we flew from Holy Cross to Kalskag, Alaska, a small village along the Kuskokwim river. Reaching Kalskag, Father went to the church and I visited with relatives. After sharing a "Mass" in the church with the village people, Father Woods sent for me and we were off to McGrath. This was in the evening about 6:30 p.m. with dusk getting ready to set in.

The trip from Kalskag to McGrath was about an hour and a half. Flying in the evening, everything looked so quite, calm with the beautiful Spring scenery. There was still a lot of snow on the mountains with frozen ice on rivers, lakes and streams. The sun was setting and dusk was falling fast, casting evening shadows everywhere.

Reaching McGrath, I was introduced to the family who were to be my employers. They were total strangers, who I was told I would live with and work for. In talking with the mom, of the kids I was to care for, she told me her sister-in-law in Fairbanks was also looking for home help. I was asked if I would like to stay in McGrath to work there, or travel to Fairbanks. Of course, being the adventure seeking person that I was, I chose to go all the way, so Fairbanks was chosen.

The next day, the brother of the Fairbanks family flew to McGrath in this "very small" plane to take me to the city. What an adventure this was. I remember it was very windy as we set out on our flying journey. The plan was big enough for two people. My suitcase was put behind the two front seats. There was barely enough room for that. The pilot controlled the plane by this small handle in the middle of his lap. This would be a scary way to travel now. But at that time, being young, I didn't worry about anything except enjoying the adventure.

We left McGrath about 10:30 a.m. that morning and traveled until we reached Lake Minchumina. Because of high winds, we stayed in that small settlement for a few hours waiting for calmer weather. The ride from McGrath to there was very rough and bouncy moving the small plane up, down and sideways.

When the pilot thought the winds calmed down a little, we took off for Nenana. The ride was still pretty bumpy, so reaching Nenana, we stayed a while waiting for calmer weather again.

After an hour or so we took off for the final leg of our journey. Fairbanks finally came to sight about an hour or so after leaving Nenana. What a rough trip that was, but enjoyable to me, being fresh from the village with no new experiences in my life. This was a great adventure.

Fairbanks seemed like a big city to me in comparison to the small village I had left behind. I was excited to be there and to meet the family I was to live with for the next year.

At the end of that summer, I was talked into attending Monroe Catholic school in Fairbanks and so I repeated my junior year of high school. Because of skipping years of school, I was older than the other students and the only "Native". This was a little scary, but meeting the kids there made it easier. They were all very friendly, kind and made me feel welcome. Since it was a catholic school, nuns were used as teachers. Some of them were a little strict but I didn't mind. It seemed like the subjects were a little hard for me and at times instead of listening to the teachers, I found myself daydreaming of home.

One thing I remember was the lockers we had for storing books and belongings. I could never open my locker and always had to have help with the combination. This was a new thing for me, and I had a hard time mastering combination locks.

At the end of that school year, around the end of May, I received a phone call from my favorite pilot "Father Woods". He was leaving for McGrath the next day and asked if I would be interested in traveling back home with him. Yes, was the answer again, from this adventure seeking kid. The next day, on a Sunday, we left Fairbanks in the small "Cessna" about 11:30 a.m. This ride to McGrath was a lot smoother than my ride the previous year to Fairbanks.

We had good weather, but had to fly through small cloud patches a few times. To break the monotony of the long trip, Father let me take the steering control a few times. I thought that was great.

We stayed in McGrath a few days which was fun to visit with old friends. I spent those days living with the family I was first introduced to the year before. Even though I enjoyed my stay in Fairbanks, it was great to be back to an area where I knew people and to be closer to home.

Then came the day Father Woods announced we were ready to travel to Holy Cross. We left McGrath late in the day, about 6:30 p.m. Traveling in the Spring gave us the advantage of more daylight. The evening and scenery was beautiful. The river ice was gone and high-water was evident everywhere. As we traveled, it seemed like there was water all around. Lakes, streams, sloughs, and rivers were all overflowing. Over some areas we could see geese flying to their own destinations.

After being away for a year, it was great to finally reach the village and home again. I was excited about that and seeing my younger brothers. It seemed like everyone grew a little since I was away and they were all shy for a while until we became reacquainted.

That summer was the last summer I spent at home. In the Fall I continued my senior year of high school and graduated in the Spring of 1963 in Holy Cross. I was the only senior graduate from that small school.

After graduating, I left the village to travel to Anchorage. There I worked for the family I was to have worked for in McGrath, the previous year before I traveled to Fairbanks.

Living in Anchorage, I attended evening business school. My thanks goes to the woman I worked for who encouraged me to attend further schooling. She was very patient with me and helped by encouraging me daily to attend further schooling. I think she worried over my future more than anyone else had in my past.

I later attended, through the Bureau of Indian Affairs, a business college in Long Beach, California. This was a good experience and adventure which I never regretted doing. After attending the school for a few months, I decided I had had enough of that.

This was a big change from living in Alaska, weather and temperature wise. It was so hot some days I couldn't stand the sweating and skin problems I had from the heat.

I got a job at McDonald Douglas Aircraft and worked there for several months before returning to Anchorage. In Anchorage, I worked for the Public Health Service as a clerk typist in the Director's office. I transferred to the hospital admitting office and later as a receptionist in the specialty clinic.

In later years, I started working for the Anchorage School District. I am presently an Elementary School Secretary, starting my 14th year at the same school.

I'm married to Angus Joseph of Beaver, Alaska, and we have five children. Three of our own, (a daughter and two sons), and two children in-laws, a daughter and son.

This ends my story of living in the village and my fishcamp adventures and travels.

I hope you enjoyed reading it as much as I have in writing it and remembering long past adventures. All that is written is from memory, not knowing about keeping diaries or notes at that time of my young life. Mom helped with her many stories and reminiscing of her and dad's early life together with grandparents.